To —
Gilbert T. Stepheson Esq

In the joy of spraying
a human orchard,

Laurence C. Jones
Piney Woods School
Piney Woods
Miss.
1962.

THE LITTLE PROFESSOR OF PINEY WOODS

Students enjoy reading in their new library and listening to storytelling.

Students learning trades while earning their way through school.

Mattie Singleton, Director of
Student Cafeteria Kitchen.

Air View of Piney Woods
Country Life School Today.

Professor Laurence C.
Jones.

→

Dr. Zilpha Ellen Chandler
who came to Piney Woods
fourteen years ago to make
the commencement address
and stayed to direct the
Academic Department.

Piney Woods Country
Life School in 1910.

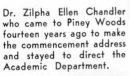

THE
LITTLE
PROFESSOR
OF
PINEY WOODS

The Story of Professor Laurence Jones

by **BETH** (Feagles) **DAY**

Julian Messner, Inc. • *New York*

Published by Julian Messner, Inc.
8 West 40th Street, New York 18
Published simultaneously in Canada
by The Copp Clark Company, Ltd.
© Copyright 1955 by Beth Day
Printed in the United States of America

Library of Congress Catalog Card No. 55-10543

Fourth Printing, 1956

Photographs by Hiatt Photo Service,
Hughes Photo-Studies, Mitchell Studio,
Claude W. Phifer, Standard Photo Co.

To my friends at Piney Woods who showed
me a world of work, laughter and of spirit.
B. D.

Contents

Foreword

On a Sunday afternoon, January 23, 1955, Jackson, Mississippi, witnessed a heartening triumph in democracy. For the first time in the history of this southern state white and colored publicly shared a speakers' platform, to pay tribute to an outstanding citizen: Dr. Laurence Clifton Jones, president and founder of the Piney Woods Country Life School.

Accolades, that Sunday afternoon, ranged from Governor Hugh White's designation of Dr. Jones as "Mississippi's First Citizen" to "Modern Moses of the Black Belt" and "Mississippi's Booker T. Washington" as white and colored leaders expressed their appreciation for the man who, for more than forty-five years, has quietly but persistently turned thousands of forgotten backwoods children into first-class citizens by providing them with an education, a home, and a new way of life.

Today the Piney Woods Country Life School, located twenty-two miles southeast of Jackson in the hill country of Rankin County, has a three-quarter-of-a-million-dollar physical plant which includes substantial brick buildings, dairies, gardens, orchards, and farm lands, as well as nearly a million dollars in permanent endowment, a regular enrollment of five hundred boarding students, and a staff of forty teachers.

Its growth, from a handful of barefoot boys in a backwoods clearing to the present impressive institution, is the story of its founder, a Missouri-born, northern-educated Negro who chose, at an age when most young men dream of financial success and personal luxuries, to come South and cast his lot with the poorest and most needy of his people.

Chapter 1

"You Is Got Yo' Paw in de Lion's Mouth"

It was a lazy, sun-drenched spring day in 1909 when a short, boyishly handsome young Negro, with skin the color of burnished mahogany, and lively, penetrating brown eyes, stepped from the Jim Crow section of a Gulf & Ship Island train at the little whistle stop of Braxton, Mississippi—a third of the way down the line from the state capital, Jackson, and the busy resort and shipping city of Gulfport.

The handful of village loungers, resting in the shade in front of Braxton's combination feed, dry goods, and grocery store straightened in surprise as they saw the young colored man. "A dressed-up nigger" was a rare enough sight in the backwoods of southern Mississippi, but the expression of alert intelligence on this young man's face, the purposeful vigor with which he strode past them, traveling bag in hand, were even more startling to an audience accustomed to the apathetic shuffle of the backwoods Negro than the well-cut city suit, high white collar, and fashionable bow tie that he wore. But even as they watched, nudging each other with whispered comment, the young man was nearly out of sight, turning with rapid steps up a side road that led from the village's dusty main street back toward the pine-covered hills.

A year in the South had taught Laurence Jones that he was an object of conjecture and often of suspicion to colored and white Southerners alike. It was for this reason that he was now hurrying up a back road, away from the speculative eyes of his onlookers. The one thing he was determined to avoid was trouble. One incident, no matter how groundless, would mean the irrevocable ruin of the dream that had brought him to these hills.

As the deeply-rutted, red-earth road led him beyond the eyes of

11

the villagers, the young man slowed his pace, breathed deeply of the southern spring, and looked around at his new home.

This was a piney woods country. Low tangles of scrub pine grew nearly to the winding roadway which was fringed at its edges by banks of wood violets. Back of the thickets loomed the tall pines, interlaced by delicate white blossoms of the dogwood and the warming flash of redbuds.

A mile or more beyond the village stretches of cleared land marked the first of small farms. One-room, windowless cabins built from hand-felled logs had grass-and-mud chimneys that at any moment might "catch," as the piney woods folk said, and take the cabins with them in flames. But bricks cost money, and this was the sparse hill-country farm area where the piney woods farmers made up a large percentage of the Negroes that constituted over half of Mississippi's total population. Most of them share-cropped poor land for barely enough to feed their families through the winter; few could read or write, an X constituting their legal mark; and the height of their ambition was to buy a little snuff and the "fixings" to have a "frolic" at Christmas.

Laurence shifted his valise from one hand to the other. In it were his worldly possessions: a few clean shirts, a Bible, copies of Wallace's *Farmer* and *Successful Farming*, and his college diploma from the University of Iowa, class of 1907. In his pocket he had a dollar and sixty-five cents, his total money wealth. With these assets, coupled with vigorous good health, an alert, eager mind, and a warm love for humanity, he intended to bring education and the chance for a better life to the illiterate colored folk of the piney woods. It was a career he had been aiming at subconsciously for the major part of his twenty-four years.

Born into the world of color, "where life begins at a discount," as a boy he had experienced relatively little of the miseries that traditionally haunt the Negro child. His father—head porter at the Pacific Hotel in St. Joseph, Missouri, and owner of the hotel barbershop—brought home a "living" which not only afforded the necessary food and shelter but also the luxury of a summer cottage. From his father—a tall, striking part-Castilian colored man—Laurence absorbed a sense of the dignity of labor and a sturdy practical outlook. To be the right man in the right place was "good enough work for anybody." As a spur to this simple acceptance of life was his mother's wistful, romantic idealism. To do your job well to this fragile, Wisconsin-born, sensitive quadroon woman was no more than your daily duty to God. Beyond that lay the infinite possibilities of greatness for him who dared.

In a childhood that held both security and popularity, the boy dreamed of an easy, gregarious adult life in which he would "run a chicken farm" which would pay the expenses for an endless round of parties, amusement, travel, and adventure. He even had the house picked out that he was to live in—a massive, friendly three-story brick at the fork of two streets which he passed daily on his newspaper route. With his busy imagination and persuasive, personable ways, which attracted the attention of both colored and white, such a life did not seem beyond attainment.

But always, shadowing the delight of such a pleasantly selfish future, hung memories he could not forget. There was the little black girl he had invited to his house for supper who ate with a mouth-stuffing greed, then explained that this was the first meal she had eaten that consisted of more than "bed and gaby" (bread and gravy). His own supper caught in his throat as he tried to picture what "bed and gaby" would be like as an everyday diet. Impulsively, he begged her to "come every night" and to bring her baby brother with her.

Then there were the tenants who rented a little house from his father. The first time he went along with his father to collect the rent money, Laurence was stunned at the squalor he witnessed. Back home he begged his parents not to charge for the month of December so that these poor people might have money for a good time at Christmas. Later, he worked for a colored doctor, making the rounds of poverty-stricken homes where he witnessed, firsthand, the misery of disease, accident, and insufficient diet.

These experiences for this boy, with his odd balance of practicality and ideals, meant more than a child's sentimental reaction to its first taste of reality. They burned in his memory not as a cause for tears but for conjecture. Why, he wondered, was he favored with an attractive face and body, a bright mind, a chance to go to school, when others—with no more choice than he about where or to whom

they had been born—were destined for crippling ugliness, for ignorance, poverty, and despair?

It was not until his junior year at the University of Iowa that
Laurence's nebulous notions fell into a working pattern.

For a seminar course in Industrial Arts the young student chose,
as his subject, Booker T. Washington. He was amazed, as he dug
into his subject, to discover how applicable the great educator's
thinking and plans were to his own vague dreams of service. Washington's theory of "putting down the bucket where you are" matched
his developing idea of service for his race. Laurence was particularly
fascinated to find that Mark Hopkins had taught General S. C.
Armstrong who, in turn, had taught Washington. Here was living
evidence of that "infinite potential" of human greatness. To be a
link in such a life-giving chain was a soul-stirring challenge.

Toward the end of that same year the president of the university,
in a routine address to the students, based his talk on that hoary old
maxim, *noblesse oblige*. To most of those in chapel that day this was
a reminder that as college men they owed a debt to society. But to
the earnest young Negro, wrestling privately with the course his life
must take, the old phrase took on fresh meaning and validity. He
had long felt the responsibility of his own advantages. That those
advantages should spell obligations to those less favored than himself
made sense. He saw it as a simple duty to take what talents and
training he had received and use them to help the "forgotten"
children of his race.

The most "forgotten" of all, he found, lived in the Black Belt of
the deep South—a country Laurence had never seen, and a country
which the colored people he had grown up with "thanked God" they
were "not from."

When he had completed the work for his degree, without explanation to either family or friends, the young graduate pawned the
watch that his Delta Tau fraternity friends (where he had waited on
the table to help pay his way through college) had given him as a
graduation present, bought a railroad ticket, and headed South.
That had been a step into the dark.

Now, as the southern country road became steeper and more
rutted, Laurence paused to rest in the shade of a spreading field
pine and wipe the sweat from his forehead and cheeks with a linen

handkerchief. From the Braxton station to the farm where he was headed was a good four-mile walk, and a relentless noon sun was taking its toll.

When he had come South the summer before Laurence had stopped in Arkansas. He smiled as he thought of the excuse he had given himself: "To get acclimated to the southern heat." Actually it had been fear, the reasonable fear of easing yourself into cold water.

An old colored woman he met soon after his arrival at Hot Springs gave succinct phrasing to his worries. "Chile," she had said, wagging a warning finger under his nose, "you is from up Norf. But now you is in de land of de *secesses*. You is got yo' paw in de lion's mouth. Now don't you be rarin' an' pitchin' to git it out. You jes' *ease* it out de bes' way you kin!"

"Easing it out," the young man soon discovered, required almost superhuman forbearance and control. But with the invincible practicality of a man who believes in his own mission, Laurence fought down the hot words and the hot blood that rose in natural reaction to the amazing and varying "taboos." He quickly learned, just as his wise old friend had warned him, that if he were to do any job in the South beyond getting himself "run out" he must know "the rules," which applied to all colored people, regardless of background. He found that the top job his college degree could command in Hot Springs was caring for a horse and cow; that all Negroes must go to the back door; that he was not to introduce himself, nor expect to be addressed as "Mister," and that he was slated with all the men of his race to the ignominious designation of "Boy," "Sam," or "George."

The most difficult of all the southern restrictions for Laurence to take was that of not speaking to a white man unless first spoken to. This was one rule he knew he would learn, only to break, when the time came. For, unlike his southern brothers, he had known white men on intimate enough terms in the past to realize that their hearts beat the same as the man of color. Brought up in a mixed community, with Jewish neighbors on one side and German on the other, he had been a community favorite as a boy, and later in Marshalltown, Iowa, where he attended high school. The first Negro graduate of the Marshalltown High School, he had been given an ovation by

the audience when he received his diploma. When he completed his
degree at the University of Iowa he had received a dozen job offers,
ranging from a subsidized career in musical comedy to a position
with an insurance firm.

But none of this seemed to matter below the Mason and Dixon's
line where all Negroes were lumped together regardless of their
education or abilities. "I could understand why anyone would want
a man with a load of manure to go to the back door," Jones later
commented, "but it was difficult for me to understand why a teacher,
minister, or businessman should do the same."

After leaving Arkansas, Laurence's next step was not exactly
easing his "paw out of de lion's mouth." He went to the Delta region,
the rich, flat northwestern part of Mississippi where wealthy plantation owners exploited both the black land and the black man. Here
share croppers worked, in terms of seeing, from "can to can't" in
cotton fields that came up to their cabin doors, bought their food
and clothing from the owner's commissary at whatever profit his
conscience dictated, and, not being able to read or "figger," accepted
on faith anything due at the end of the year.

Laurence quickly found that "sublime" ignorance was what the
plantation owners wanted. "Educate the niggers? Hell, no. What we
want from them is that cotton and no sass." Nor did he receive any
more encouragement from the Negroes themselves. "If we ask questions we is cussed," explained one old farmer, "and if we raises up—
we is beat up or shot!"

Laurence had sense enough to realize that he was outmatched.
The Delta would have to wait. Dejected and broke, he headed
South to the small farm area. With winter coming on he took a job
teaching at a small school in Hinds County, Mississippi. At
Christmas he went home with one of his students to spend the holi-
days in Rankin County and had his first taste of the piney woods.

This was a world apart from the Delta country. Here small farmers,
both white and colored, were caught in a subsistence-level economy.
Only a few inadequate schools existed for the whites and practically
none for the colored. It was a land of ignorance and superstition,
of a starvation-level existence. Here was a practicing belief in
"voodooism" and the "conjuh" men; graves were decorated with
broken bits of colored glass; crops were planted when the moon was

right; and most of life was lived in accordance with primitive taboos. He remembered vividly the crowning experience of that Christmas which strengthened a growing desire to cast his lot among the people of the piney woods.

Through the great dark woods by the light of a pine torch he was taken to a frolic. In a close room, filled with tobacco smoke and reeking with the odor of whisky, a crowd of men, women, and children, laughing and joking, jostled and danced to the music of an old guitar until early morning. Occasionally a man would step outside and with a succession of shots satisfy himself as to how quickly he could pull the trigger of his pistol.

The children seemed to participate in the frolic quite as much as the older people. They swore just as wickedly, and even the boys and girls nine years of age used quantities of snuff and tobacco. Their parents thought that anything, even liquor, if used by themselves, was all right for the children; so it was only necessary to ask "Pa" for what was wanted. Around the corners of the room the babies were dumped in the laps of women too old to dance.

It was the pathetic gaiety of bitter poverty; it was the one time of the year when the people let go and literally "shot the works." The Christmas frolic lasted for a full month, moving from cabin to cabin, exhausting all that had been saved in provisions and in spending all available money for fireworks, cheap jewelry, perfume, whisky, tobacco, and for the "makings" of pies and cakes that weighed heavily on stomachs flattened by the corn-pone and cowpea diet of the previous eleven months.

Here, young Jones realized, was the beginning point for education. The nickels and dimes that went for this heart-sickening waste —the waste of desperation and ignorance—if saved would mean the difference between not having and having meat on the table during the year, whitewash for the cabin, books and education, and the beginnings toward a better life. To supply that missing hope seemed to him the mission that he had been looking for.

Laurence talked to many of them individually that night of his first frolic—passionately and eagerly—and they listened with native courtesy but kept their reaction hidden behind the veiled withdrawal of their eyes. He found that there were a couple of schools for Negroes in the county which, if a child could get in, did not go beyond the eighth grade. There was no high school, although a church association had been trying to build one for twenty-five years.

The next day, while the frolic continued its uninterrupted frenzy, Laurence borrowed a mule from his host and went to look at the two school buildings. They were one-room structures with no windows and no blackboards—the only available facilities for many thousands of colored children. The two teachers who had finished only the fifth grade themselves were paid $18 a month for a three- or four-months period. Their pupils came in from miles around when not needed for work on the farms, and were of all ages. The cold "tater" that they brought for lunch did their stomachs about as much good as what they learned did their minds.

Like Booker T. Washington before him, the young man realized that education for these impoverished people must begin with the simple problem of survival—of how to raise sufficient food to feed their families; how to do a more skilled job than chopping cotton.

Though his own college work had been in Liberal Arts, Laurence had always had a feeling for practical education. His childhood hero, Robinson Crusoe, had made a deep impression because he had "made things to suit his needs" and in imitation of him the boy had built many back-yard coops and shelters, raised chickens and pigeons, and made a garden. In Iowa he had been fascinated by the accent on thrifty farming and the many agricultural developments.

On the last night of the frolic Laurence rounded up the group of celebrants—men, women, and children—and as they sat outside the cabin, around a huge pine-knot fire, he told them about Christmas and how it was celebrated in Iowa and Missouri—a solemn festival to our Lord with simple homemade gifts of fruit or candy and an accent on the spirit of "Christmas and the Christly example of brotherhood and love." He spoke of the farms of Iowa, where thrifty farmers raised food crops for their families to eat during the long winter months, where they varied their crops, planted wisely, and made enough so that they could educate their children. He told them he would like to come back and help them with their farms and crops and the education of their children so that they could look forward to a life like that.

Perhaps some of the men may have wanted to laugh at this slim young man standing there before them with his earnest eyes and big dreams, but with the childlike perception of simple folk, they knew his heart was right. So with simple dignity they thanked him for his talk, prayed that he might be "spared," and when he departed, no doubt expected to see no more of him.

But the memory of those firelit faces had burned too bright in Laurence's mind and heart. As soon as he got back to Hinds County, he sent to Iowa for books on agriculture, pamphlets, from the Iowa Corn Growers' Association and the Wallace experimentations, as well as government brochures on rural sanitation and rural economy, and each night, after classes, he studied these basic lessons in farm life—in preparation for his new job.

And now he was back and ready to begin.

Chapter 2

"Jes' a-Lookin' for a Home"

> Boll Weevil say to de Preacher,
> You better close you' chu'ch do',
> When I git through wid de Farmer,
> He cain't pay de Preacher no mo'.
> Jes' a-looking for a home, jes'
> a-lookin' for a home.
> —*De Ballit of De Boll Weevil*

"Lawdy, if it ain't the little 'Fesser!"

Amon Gibson's genial brown face shone with hospitable welcome as he saw the young man trudging up the path toward his cabin. He clambered down the porch steps, walked out to meet Laurence, his hand stretched forth in greeting.

"You said you was comin' back!"

Laurence set his little bag down on the front gallery of the cabin and shook hands with the farmer.

"Yes, I'm back." He smiled. "Back to stay. Will it be all right if I live at your place for a while?"

"All right!" Amon laughed and clapped a broad hand on the younger man's shoulder. "Why, 'Fesser, Ah'd give you the breast of the Sunday chicken and a fresh-filled feather bed jes' to have you to visit with us of an evenin'." He cupped his hand to his mouth, let out a "holler" in the direction of the back yard, and smiled again. "Jes' wait till Martha fin's you're hyear—won't she be pleased!"

Amon Gibson was the "second most prosperous" colored farmer in the community and Laurence came to him because he had sensed his warm hospitality and sweet spirit on his visit the Christmas before. "Second most prosperous" farmer meant that Amon, in contrast to the share-cropping farmers, owned his land and, in addi-

20

tion, a team of strapping gray mules with which he did his plowing and cultivating and used to pull his wagon when he went to town or to church on Sunday. With a surcingle and a folded meal sack strapped around their straight backs, the mules also doubled as "riding horses" when it was wet or muddy and on roads—more correctly trails—that were too narrow and winding for the wagon.

The most prosperous farmer of the community was a taciturn ex-slave, Ed Taylor who, according to local legend, had lived up North after the war long enough to "git eddicated and git mean." He had come back to Mississippi, bought up farm land, and made enough out of it to loan money as a business. Uncle Ed, as he was called, kept to himself, and Laurence had not met him on his Christmas visit. He had been told, however, that the old man, who had been known to " 'close" a mortgage, was no man to deal with.

"So you's fixin' to sta't a school," Amon mused, when the two men were comfortably settled on split cane-bottomed chairs on the porch while waiting the call to supper. "I'm mighty glad to see you and have you for a visit, but I don't know about a school." He scratched his head thoughtfully. "You know we've had us a chu'ch 'sociation roun' hyear for nigh onto twenty-five years a-tryin' to do the same thing——"

"I know," Laurence broke in eagerly, "but everyone seems to have given up hope. I think I know a way we can really get a school going. I'm here to do the teaching and to run it. That much is taken care of. Now what we've got to do is raise money for a building."

"Ah hates to say it"—Amon shook his head again—"but that's a biggah problem than you think fo'."

"I realize no one has much money to give," Laurence admitted, "but the school would serve two counties. There are thousands of families living in this area. If each one of them could give a little, then we would have at least enough to begin. That's what I want to do this summer—travel all over this part of the country and tell everyone about the school and what I plan to do. By fall I should have raised enough to start."

Amon glanced at his young friend with shrewd eyes. "You think white folks is goin' to let you sta't a cull'ud school?"

"I'm going to them first and tell them what I plan to do. I'll get their permission before I begin. If they understand what I want to do, some of them might help."

"He'p!" Amon snorted. "You'll be lucky if they let you stay 'round hyear, let alone he'p."

"Well," Laurence said, "we'll see. All I need from them is their permission. If I can get enough money from the colored people this summer to get started, I might be able to raise money back North to keep the school going this winter. There are lots of folks there who would like to see a thing like this work out down here."

"White folks?" Amon asked curiously.

"White folks and colored, too. But I've got to start with the colored down here. If they aren't willing to back their own school, nobody else is going to be."

"It ain't that." Amon sighed. "It's jes' you come at the wrong time—"

"What do you mean by wrong time?"

"Boll weevil got hyear firs'."

Amon looked out thoughtfully across his own ragged cotton patch toward the deep woods, hitched his chair back against the wall of the house, and said slowly, "Few years ago you might-a been able to stir up a little cash 'mongst us folks, 'Fesser. But Mr. Boll Weevil, he's got us all licked now. Ain't nobody got any money a-tall 'round' hyear."

On his first trip out into the country around, on the following Sunday, astride one of Amon's mules, Laurence began to understand just what the farmer meant. The group that he spoke to at a little country church listened—some with pathetic eagerness—while he described his plans for starting a school. But when the collection was taken up for the building only thirty cents was contributed by the forty-two members of the congregation.

Riding back toward the Gibson farm, Laurence turned over the prospects in his mind. What Amon had told him about the boll weevil was only too true. The young teacher had managed to hit the piney woods just about the same time as the little bug which, having eaten its way up from Mexico, through the cotton patches of Texas and Arkansas and Louisiana, in its steady march of forty miles a year, had made its devastating appearance in the fields of southern Mississippi. For the one-crop farmer, who bought his "meat

and meal" all year long on credit against his cotton crop, Mr. Boll
Weevil spelled disaster. Over the cotton country shrewd storekeepers
began watching the fields around and, "Nothin' doin', boy, you got
weevils in your field," sounded its echo of starvation over the land.

The few dollars the small farmers might have invested in a school
had dwindled to a few pennies.

That one-crop farming was one of the things Laurence hoped to
combat. There was little point worrying about teaching Latin and
higher mathematics to people who had not yet solved the problems
of day-to-day livelihood. His "night course" in agriculture, coupled
with an observant eye, made the immediate necessities obvious: they
must learn how to raise food crops as well as cotton; how to plow
so that the rains wouldn't wash away the thin topsoil; how to clean
up their cabins and store their food so that it would not spoil; how
to develop pride in the ordinary labor that constituted their lives;
how to be thrifty. These were the things they must be taught first.

A smile crossed Laurence's face as he considered this job he was
setting up for himself: a job of soap and whitewash, fertilizer and
seed. It was a far cry from the things he had enjoyed most as a boy:
music, poetry, books, the theater. The job he had loved best was that
of passing glasses of water to patrons of the local theater between
acts, for which he received not only pay, but the inestimable delight
of watching the "greats" of the legitimate stage: Sir Henry Irving,
Ellen Terry, and Richard Mansfield. He thought of the night, after
a rousing performance of *The Count of Monte Cristo,* when, carried
away by the exciting drama, he and another boy had gone out into
the alley back of the theater and fenced with canes.

From dueling to muleback—perhaps it was not such a bad switch
after all. He was lucky to have a mule, Laurence decided. He would
need it, and any other transportation he could borrow, to carry his
message to the woods people.

Next morning, armed with a dollar of his scant funds, Laurence
set out to meet the leaders of the white community. First he went to
the Braxton Bank, where he opened an account with the dollar, and
thereby was able to meet the officers of the little bank: R. F. Everett,
J. P. Cox, and Wiley Mangum. All three men listened courteously to
his story. Particularly in the young cashier, Wiley Mangum, Laurence sensed a sympathetic ally.

From Braxton, Laurence headed back toward Comby, a little sawmill settlement between Braxton and the Gibson farm which was owned and operated by John Webster, who, Laurence had found, was a key figure in the immediate community.

As he trudged up the trail toward Comby, when the mill buildings, combination post office, and general store came into view, a chill settled over the young man's heart, causing him to shiver, although he walked under a warm sun. Then he came to a sudden halt.

Before him, over the post office, an American flag rose and dipped in the spring wind. Staring up at it, as it spread grandly before him, Laurence swallowed with the dry throat of remembered terror, then moved slowly forward, his luminous eyes fixed in the grip of a long-ago memory.

He could never see the Stars and Stripes lift in a breeze without thinking, with a repetition of the fear that had gripped him as a child, of the one-and-only time he had ever seen his father cry.

It had been a warm, friendly morning not unlike this. He was walking with his father toward the Pacific Hotel, and just as they passed the post office the American flag over the building, caught by a gust of wind, whipped out over their heads in grand silken majesty.

Entranced by the brilliant stripes streaming in the wind, the five-year-old boy was suddenly startled by a strange sound and, turning, saw his tall, usually calm father standing motionless beneath the flag, tears pouring unheeded down his dark cheeks as he stared with unseeing eyes at those streaming folds. Then his father cried out in a strange, shaken voice his small son had never heard before, "Stand by, Old Glory! Don't make no difference if they lynches a black man every day for forty years! We can stand it—us black folks—we can stand it against the day of reckoning! Old Glory's still a-waving! Reckon she's going to be the shelter and covering for a cussed thing like that forever! No, no, by God!" His clenched fist struck his son's shoulder, spinning the terrified child against a stone wall.

As he clung to the cold stone, sobbing in a mixture of sympathy and terror, Laurence thought of the story in the newspaper which his father and mother had discussed that morning at breakfast with hushed voices and ashen faces.

It was a scene Laurence could not recall without that childish

chill that had gripped his heart then as it did now. Perhaps it was
that which had brought him here now to help his people.

"What-ya want, Sam?"

Laurence shook off the tenacious reverie, looked around at a
ragged teenager who was examining him with curious, though not
unfriendly, blue eyes.

"I want to see Mr. Webster," Laurence said.

"Foreman in the mill does the hirin'," replied the boy, eying with
frank fascination Laurence's tight-fitting single-breasted suit and
high white collar.

"My name is Jones," Laurence explained, sensing that the boy's
questions were prompted by a desire to be helpful, "and I'd like to
see Mr. Webster on personal business."

"Well, Jones," the boy said confidentially, "I'm a-tellin' you now
that Mr. Webster—I works fo' him—he's a high-toned man. If you
go see him you better speak right up soon as he lets you and get
out fast and don't waste no time!"

"Thanks for the advice," Laurence said, with an amused smile.

Something in the warmth of the young colored man's smile
caught the boy's off-southern side. "I'm Wilk Kelly," he said, some-
what uncertainly.

"I'm glad to meet you, Mr. Kelly," Laurence said gravely. "Now
which way is Mr. Webster's office?"

"Right thoo there." The towheaded boy pointed out a door at the
side of the building. Laurence nodded thanks and went in.

John Webster was sitting at his desk, his back to the door. His
secretary, Miss Nannie Simmons, was at a typing desk on one side,
and his bookkeeper, Albert Howell, at the opposite end of the room.
When the young colored man walked into the office, the two employees looked up in startled surprise.

"Mr. Webster?"

John Webster peered around, satisfied that it was just a nigger,
grunted, "Well?" and went back to his work.

"Mr. Webster, I'm Laurence Jones."

Webster's head shot up and he turned around to face his visitor.
A barely audible "Well, I never!" escaped Miss Nannie's lips. It was
the first time any of the three in that office had ever heard a Negro
introduce himself.

"I've come here to start a school for colored children," Laurence said crisply, "an agricultural-industrial school to teach better farming practices and trades."

He paused a second while Webster eased back in his chair and grunted a second, "Well?"

Laurence could feel the tension in the room as the three Southerners found themselves in the unfamiliar and uncomfortable position of "listening to a nigger" talk. Laurence spoke rapidly, and to the point, outlining his plan for the school and what he intended to do. He kept his penetrating eyes fixed on John Webster's heavy-set but well-featured face. As he spoke Laurence noted that the man's intelligent dark eyes flickered interest that indicated he followed all that was said. But when he had finished, Webster's answering voice was flat.

"No use trying to start a colored school here, Jones. We white folks have enough trouble supportin' schools for ourselves."

"I'm not asking you for money," Laurence said quietly. "I only want your permission and advice."

"My advice to you is to give up such an idea," Webster said. "You won't get any help out of the whites."

"Will I get any hindrance?"

Webster shrugged. "Not from me. I don't care what you do. I won't ever lift a hand to stop you."

"What about the others?"

"I can't speak for the others."

"Will you tell me whom I should see?"

"I s'pose so," Webster grunted.

Laurence whipped out a pad and pencil, held the pencil poised, waiting. Faced with such unfamiliar persistence, John Webster shifted uncomfortably in his chair.

"Well, there's Bob Hemphill, Anderson Pruitt, William Pattie, Gabe Jones, and Eddie Ammons right around here," he said. "Then you be sure and go down to Braxton and talk to the bankers—and the Barwick Brothers, and Mrs. Caline Barwick."

"Thank you, Mr. Webster." Laurence snapped his notebook shut, pocketed it, and bowed. "May I call on you again?"

"Reckon so," Webster mumbled uneasily, "but I'm a-tellin' you,

Jones, I'm a heap more interested in sawmilling than I am in nigger education."

The crescendo of nervous laughter, breaking the strain under which the three Southerners had labored, that followed his exit did not disturb Laurence. He felt, instead, a glow of satisfaction. He had not only introduced himself, but he had talked eye to eye with a white man and that man had listened. Laurence made up his mind that he was going to bank a good deal on John Webster's help.

The next day Laurence discovered that Webster had given him a good list. They were all substantial members of the community, who, despite their southern background, listened with interest to his story. None of them, however, would promise actively to support the project or donate any money to it. But the main thing was that they all agreed: "If you do what you say you are going to do, we will not stand in your way."

With his first fences up in the Braxton community, Laurence headed back into the woods.

Chapter 3

"Who Dat?"

Laurence's plan for the summer was to cover as much of Rankin and Simpson counties as he could, and to speak to any group of people he could find—at churches, at frolics, or at meetings of any kind, even a small group resting under a tree at noontime from their work.

Choosing as his texts "My People Were Destroyed for Want of Knowledge" and "Ye Shall Know the Truth and the Truth Shall Make Ye Free," he started out over the back-country trails, going from cabin to cabin, country church to services held under groves— sometimes on muleback, sometimes by oxcart, more often afoot, walking eighteen and twenty miles a day, carrying his message of better living, better corn, better stock, better poultry, and the need for a school that would teach these things. He attacked the folly of using the poorest land for the corn crop from which the farm families derived their food staple; he pointed out the foolishness of using any poor ear of corn left at the bottom of the crib in the spring to plant for the next crop.

At night Laurence sat with the farmers on their porches, or around their fireplaces, and figured before their astonished eyes the cost of raising low-price cotton and buying high-priced corn and bacon from the North. He shouldered his way into the kitchens and talked to the doubting turbaned women the value of soap and whitewash, the economy of learning to preserve the summer yield from their gardens and the wild berries that grew at their door for food during the winter. He made up pails of whitewash and showed them how to whiten up their cabins—inside and out—not only for the improved appearance but to keep down pests and bugs that thrived in the unfinished logs. Often he clambered up on rickety sawhorses and boxes to start the job of whitewashing himself.

Before one group of backwoods folks who had commented admiringly on his polished speech and manner of dressing Laurence began a second address with, *"Esse quid hoc dicam vivis quod fama negatur et sua quod rarus tempora lector amat?"* Then, as they nodded in delighted and self-deprecating wonder at such scholarship, he lashed out, "What does that sentence in Latin really mean to you or to me? Does it earn my living? Does it put meat on my table? No, it's nothing but showoff. Our problem, yours and mine, is to find how to make the most of our land and our gardens so that we can eat all year round. We must learn how to do jobs well, so that folks will hire us."

With that he whipped out a copy of Wallace's *Farmer* and read to them practical advice on raising better food crops and the necessity for more sanitary conditions around a farm.

The Piney Woods folk watched their young evangelist with a mingling of admiration, good humor, and suspicion.

"I wish that feller 'ud go away," said one old farmer. "He's got too much sense. I know he's never come way down hyear with all his sense for any good to us."

Though he slept in their cabins, worked in their fields, ate at their tables, and prayed with them in church, this sort of suspicion followed him wherever he went. They had never before known a "foreigner" to come into their midst—white or black—for any good purpose.

One day, as he finished what he thought was a powerful speech, Laurence saw an old man directly in front of him nudge his neighbor and say, "That boy don't want nothin' but a dime and when he gits his dime he'll go 'way."

That he was a curiosity there was no doubt. As he made his rounds through the backwoods communities, along the country trails, muleback or afoot, he was always conscious that the woods had "eyes." If he turned quickly he could almost invariably catch a glimpse of dark heads disappearing behind thickets. Often he saw children's slim brown bodies parting the low bushes as they scurried away from him, and the low chatter of voices or stifled laughter told him that they were giving vent to their curiosity. Though their innate gentle manners kept them from laughing in his face, Laurence often caught the gleam of amusement in many an old farmer's eyes as he stood before them, speaking with boyish eagerness on matters that they thought they knew more about than he.

Perhaps if he were older or larger. . . . He was not only short and slender, Laurence realized, as one day he knelt over a clear-running stream to get a drink of water, but his face was ridiculously boyish for the mission he was attempting to accomplish. He stared critically at his reflection in the water. A smooth-cheeked young face dominated by wide, magnetic eyes. A silghtly aquiline nose, high forehead, and curling black hair. The upper part of his face was all right, the young man decided. It was his mouth that betrayed him: long, curving, sensitive lips—the mouth of a dreamer, the mouth of a child. He turned his head sidewise till he could get a profile reflection, felt of the back of his neck where it curved in, smooth and vulnerable as a baby's. Maybe he should let his hair grow long to fill in that hollow. And a mustache. How would that be? Laurence placed his small, tapering hand over his lips and studied the reflection. Yes, a mustache would help. With his mouth and neck covered up he might look more dignified. He sighed. How did he expect grown men to take him seriously when he looked as though he was barely out of those velveteen knee pants his mother used to dress him in?

Colored people, even more than others, believed that age was a necessary adjunct to knowledge. Laurence thought of the time when it had first entered his brain that young men were capable of doing a big job.

Dissatisfied with the education he was getting at St. Joseph High School, Laurence had visited an uncle in Marshalltown, Iowa, had liked the city, and had gotten a job in a hotel to pay his expenses and entered high school there. Both the superintendent of schools and the high school principal were young men under thirty, and were making a definite impact upon the community. Laurence had been particularly impressed with the principal, Ellis Graff, a teacher with enthusiasm and imagination, who had always taken time to talk with and encourage the young Negro student.

Then, later, there had been a young woman, too, who had impressed him with the job she was doing. It was after his seminar report on Booker T. Washington as a junior in the University of Iowa, and he had been asked to make a speech at a church in downtown

Iowa City. In his audience that night was a young colored woman, Grace Allen, who was in town in her job as solicitor for a Kentucky college called Eckstein-Norton. When Laurence had finished, Miss Allen was called upon to add what she could to the picture of the Negro in the South. Laurence had been startled when the small, vigorous, bright-eyed young woman rose and launched into a speech that was both stirring and inspirational. He had decided then and there that Miss Allen was the brightest and most enthusiastic woman of his race that he had ever met. Privately he had determined that someday they would meet again—someday when he, too, was doing a big job.

Well, he had better be at it. Laurence rose from the creek bank, dusted off his knees, and glanced around. This was a new section of the Piney Woods and he was not certain where he was. Vaguely, he was heading in the direction of the next Negro settlement, though he was not sure how far that would be.

As he plodded down the road he saw outlines of buildings in the distance. It was already late in the afternoon and he had not eaten since morning. But as he drew nearer he realized that they were houses, not cabins, and this meant a white settlement. He hurried on past. Beyond these few scattered houses he paused beside a tangle of wild blackberry vines, picked a handful of ripe berries, and munched them as he walked along. Then, rounding a curve in the rutted road, he saw more buildings, but even as he saw them, his heart sank. White again. He looked up at the sky with a worried frown. The sun was sinking fast—much faster than he liked. He scurried on past two white farmhouses, then slowed down to get his breath. Mile followed weary mile, and with approaching twilight came hunger and exhaustion, and still no sign of a Negro cabin. He must have missed his road and wandered by mistake into Smith County, where there were but few colored settlements. Nevertheless, he did not know what else to do but push on.

As the sun slipped to a faint glimmer on the horizon and dusk shadowed the warm summer sky, Laurence came upon still another settlement which was white. He paused a second before he went on, looking down the road, sizing up how far he must go to clear this little cluster of houses, and fear closed his throat, a strange fear that he had learned only this summer, but familiar to the southern Negro who knows that all Negroes are suspect at night, that a glib tongue or a college education is no armor against random shots or the cry, "Nigger, what are you doing here?"

Laurence stared at the little row of houses, the first lamps of evening gleaming at the windows, a sight that should have been comforting and pleasant for a traveler, and he marveled that those warm, lighted windows and signs of comfort should spell fear for him. He thought of all his white friends and how strange it was that their familiar individual faces should melt into this faceless pattern of danger. He took a deep breath, ducked his head, and started walking swift and noiselessly down the road past the houses, praying that no stray dog should by a bark announce his presence.

As he cleared the last lighted window, Laurence plunged into the black covering of the woods, then leaned against a tall pine to rest. He was trembling, cold sweat stood on his temples.

He was learning now, as his father had learned before him, what it was to "feel like a colored man."

When he had gotten his breath and his quick-beating heart had slowed down, he made his way deeper into the comforting protection of the black woods. This, to him, was another wonder. That a black, unknown woods could mean safety. City bred, Laurence had never heard the night sounds nor looked upon the writhing shadows of moving trees in the moonlight without a trace of uneasiness. But this summer had taught him many things, among them that the woods is the black man's friend.

As the wind rose, stirring the tall pines to a moaning, melodic whisper, Laurence thought of Aunt Liza, the old colored woman in whose care his mother had left him many times as a child—Bible-loving Aunt Liza whose eerie singing would rouse him from a childhood nap and he would awake, his spine prickling, to listen to her weird old voice "agonizing" in prayer. If the night was wild or dreary, if the wind was high, she would raise her voice with it, ending each hymn with a mournful, haunting query:

> "And am I a-borned toooo die,
> To a-lay this a-body down?"

At another time, without warning, she would cast her old mesmeric eyes on some golden future, unseen by the child beside her, and sing rapturously:

> "Jes' look a yander a-what I see
>   Hise de window, let de dove come in;
> A ban' of angels a-comin' for me—
>   Oh! hise de window, let de dove come in."

Many a time the little boy had stared, with fixed fascination, at the window waiting for that dove, only finally to give up when sleep overtook him.

Trudging beneath the moaning pines, seeing no sign of human life before him, Laurence considered lying down on the edge of the trail and resting his tired muscles till dawn. But the thought of the poisonous copperheads and rattlesnakes that infested the woods drove him on.

Then in what seemed an endless march—though perhaps no more than an hour's walk past the last white settlement—he made out, in a clearing ahead of him, the outlines of a one-room cabin from which the firelight flickered unevenly through the unchinked logs. An open door and the odor of burning pine mingled with the sweetish scent of hearth-baked corn bread. If this were a Negro cabin, he would be all right; if not . . .

He hurried forward, calling out as he neared the open door. A dead silence greeted his hail, then a cautious black head peered around the door-frame. The familiar, heart-warming low query rang out in the still night air,

"Who dat?"

For Laurence, his knees buckling from exhaustion, his body weak from lack of food and the drenching aftermath of fear, those were the sweetest words he had ever heard. Two words that meant unquestioning hospitality, shared food, and the promise of rest.

Cowpeas and corn bread—and a touching generosity. It was this spirit that made the young man swear to himself, once again, that he would bring help to these simple, sincere children of the woods— God willing.

Chapter 4

"Trouble Is So High"

At the end of the summer, when Laurence returned to Amon Gibson's farm, he found that his assets added up to the dollar he had in the Braxton bank, a new set of muscles, a mustache, and long hair. On the liability side his only suit was torn by the brush and the soles of his shoes were almost gone. Though he had contacted thousands of people and stirred up a lot of interest in his project he was no nearer to a school than the spring before when he arrived. Then, to make matters worse, rain had set in and, before it stopped, what the boll weevils had left of the cotton crop was ruined.

Laurence brushed up his weather-beaten suit and went to see Wiley Mangum at the bank in Braxton. Mangum greeted him with a kindly smile but with bleak words. "The worst crop year in the history of Rankin County," he said. "My money is all out, the darkies are blue, and I am blue, too. So we're all about one color."

There was little chance for help here for the little 'fesser and his school.

As Laurence helped Amon pick the few remaining bolls on the stunted stalks, he wondered if the farmer was not right. Perhaps this was the wrong year, after all. People had enough problems thinking about how they would eat for the winter. The very thought caused him to straighten up. That, he decided, was exactly *why* they must have a school. If he could get some of these boys trained in the right kind of farming this fall, next year they might be able to have some good corn on hand to carry them through the winter.

Laurence had always had his eye on the North as one of the chief sources for the funds that he would need to operate a private school in this poverty-stricken country. He had many friends in college who had shown a deep interest in the South and who had enough money to enable them to help. He had worked with and studied under teachers and businessmen who, he felt certain, would lend a sympathetic ear and open their pocketbooks to the needs of his project. But he had not wanted to ask them to help until he had something definite to point to. It took a lot of nerve to ask for help for a school that was not yet even open, but there was no other answer. Laurence sighed, leaned over a low, stunted cotton plant, and as he looked at it he realized that it was either get help—or quit.

That evening he got out pen and paper from his little bag and began writing letters. When he had fifty written, he began to address them—and then hesitated. Most of these appeals were to businessmen. It would be much better to type the addresses—at least make the letters look neat and businesslike on the outside.

Laurence remembered the typewriters he had seen at John Webster's sawmill office. Although he had not talked to the man any more, he had passed him several times on the road and the mill-owner had always greeted him in a friendly manner. Perhaps he would not mind letting him use his typewriter to address the letters.

Laurence found out that the sawmill office was closed for two hours each day at noon. Next day he was there as Webster and his two office employees were leaving. He showed Webster his package of letters.

"I would like to get these out in the next mail, Mr. Webster," he said. "I was wondering if you would mind if I addressed them on one of your typewriters."

Miss Nannie's jaw dropped with such a ludicrous expression of surprise that the bookkeeper snickered.

"Go ahead," Webster said, pointing to the nearest desk. "The typewriter is there. Go ahead and use it."

Laurence thanked him and sat down to work. He did not notice, as he slipped an envelope into the machine, that the three had stopped at the door to watch him.

"When he hit that keyboard it was like a hundred wild geese flying South," Webster later described what happened. "I thought Miss Nannie would faint."

The two employees were amazed. But not John Webster. He had already made up his mind that he was not going to be surprised at anything this young man did.

A few days later Laurence heard that the Spring Hill Church Association was to hold its annual meeting during the last two days in August at a place twenty miles from the Gibson farm. Each congregation in the association was to be represented by two members and to contribute four dollars in money which was to be divided, according to the vote of the association, among home missions, foreign missions, and superannuated ministers. His experience so far had given Laurence little hope that he would receive any help from the churches, but this might be a good audience to which to make his final appeal for help. The Gibsons, although they were not going this year, assured him that the assembly, next to the Christmas frolic, was the biggest social event of the year. Families came from long distances, many of them camping out for the entire meeting, sleeping in their tents, in their wagons, or on the ground.

The association had more than a spiritual flavor. It was a time for courting, for frolicking, for feasting. It also meant some good soul-stirring preaching for those too old to enjoy the fun. If possible, it meant a new dress for the girls and a new suit, or at least a new shirt, for the boys. It was a good time for the young folks to look over that year's matrimonial crop and see what was coming along besides the boy or the girl on the next farm.

"It's a 'sperience, I'm tellin' you," Amon said when Laurence hesitated. "You needs to have some fun." His round black eyes twinkled with remembered pleasure.

" 'Sides," chimed in Martha, "it'll give you a chance to talk to lots of folks."

Laurence caught a ride to the association grounds with a young acquaintance who had borrowed a horse and a wagon from a nearby farmer.

As the old wagon trundled down gullies and washed-out bits of road, only to "hist" alarmingly as they rolled over a root or stump, Laurence wondered about how much money would be left for education after the missionaries had taken their toll, and if there was any left, what chance he had of getting any of it. That would depend on how many of the friends he had made during the summer showed up and how hard they talked for his cause.

Finally the tired old bundle of bones pulled the creaking wagon out into a clearing in the center of which was a little log church.

This was the hub—the bull's-eye—from which swarmed all sorts of busy activity. Circling it, in a great, tempting, odorous ring, were tables loaded with hot fish, soda pop, fresh apples and oranges, cakes, pies, candies, and bread. The older people were in the church or bunched outside around its walls talking about their crop failures and their plans for the next year.

Out beyond the rows of tempting tables the girls in their fresh calicoes walked hand in hand with shy, self-conscious, white-eyed glances as they passed knots of bashful boys in stiff new suits who began walking in the opposite direction to the girls. Soon the walking would cease, choices would be made, and the serious business of courting would get under way.

Forming still another circle beyond the strolling youngsters were rows of wagons, buggies, horses, and mules. It would not be long until each vehicle would have on the seat a couple with heads together, dreaming dreams and holding hands, with the complete approval of their elders.

At a considerable distance from the animals and wagons was the inevitable adjunct to a meeting of this sort—horse traders, bootleggers, con-game men—just far enough removed from the church itself so as not to bring down the wrath of the righteous but close enough to pick off any unwary and unsuspecting "customer."

Laurence glanced over this hastily amassed community of love, liquor, and religion, and wondered what it would all mean to him. He was not long in doubt. When he presented himself to the moderator and other officers of the association, he was greeted with a cold, collective stare. Nevertheless, he briefly explained why he was there. He told them he would like to tell about his plans to the assembly.

"How do we know you won't preach?" one of them asked.

"I don't want to preach," Laurence protested. "I'm a teacher. I want to talk to the people about building a school for their children."

"We been trying to build a school for twenty-five years now," said one man, contemptuously eying the young man's city suit and youthful face. "How come you figger you can come in here and do it?"

"I can't do it without your help," Laurence said, "and that is why I want a hearing—a chance to tell all of you my plans."

For once Laurence found all of his persuasive efforts dissipated on a stone wall.

"We got business to take care of—no time for talking school," was the verdict as they walked away, leaving him to himself.

None of the friends Laurence had made during the summer were there. Then, when the actual meetings began, he found, to his amazement, that not only was he not permitted to speak but that he was not allowed to participate in any of the sessions. Everywhere he turned he met the same suspicious stares. The seeds of distrust had been well sowed by the jealous or the suspicious, he did not know which.

That night Laurence tried to locate the young fellow he had come with. He could not find him nor was he made welcome by any of the various groups that gathered in little groups. He spent a dismal night curled up at the base of a large pine tree.

Next day, although it was still August, he was completely "frozen" out by the directors, who felt he was muscling in on their territory. As soon as the business was over the whole camp became alive with people who were leaving. Individuals and families hustled about, getting their belongings together, loading their wagons, saddling and harnessing horses and mules. Again Laurence searched for his companion but there was no trace of him, of the wagon, or of the horse. He finally had his answer.

"Don't you know?" a man asked. "The boy left yes'tiddy morning, right after the old horse keeled over and died."

"Died!"

Through Laurence's mind flashed a quick picture of the old rawboned horse the boy had driven, then the long, hot twenty miles. His mind had been on other things, and he realized that he should have made the boy stop to water, feed, and let the horse rest, particularly since the old horse was fresh off pasture. Colic, probably. But right now he had to get back to Braxton. He decided to swallow his pride, in spite of the cold shoulder he had been getting, and ask for a ride. He went from wagon to wagon, but, oddly enough, no one seemed to be going his way.

Sick at heart, tired, and hot, Laurence headed wearily afoot down the rutted dusty wagon road toward Amon Gibson's. He got there, finally, just as he had gotten through woods, over streams, and from settlement to settlement all summer long. But when he arrived it was almost as if he were facing a repetition of the association's freeze. Amon's kind face registered keen concern. His other friends greeted him with the barest of civility, a few of them with open disapproval.

The news of the death of the horse had preceded his arrival. It seemed that since his companion was just a boy, Laurence was being held responsible for what had happened.

Amon advised him to go see the owner of the horse. That man left no doubt about his stand. "You owes me $175," he told Laurence.

"That's ridiculous!" Laurence exploded. "That old plug wasn't worth ten——"

"You owes me $175," repeated the farmer stubbornly, "and I wants it soon!"

Stifling an urge to tell the man just what he thought of such an outrageous charge, Laurence muttered, "I'll see about it," and stormed off down the road. Almost unconsciously he found himself heading for an isolated clearing in the woods not far from the Gibson farm where he had gone many times when he wanted to be alone—to muse and to think. Once it had been a farm. Now the long-deserted cabin, half-hidden by tall weeds, furnished shelter for a few sheep. But there was a spring of cold water and a giant spreading cedar tree for shade. The spot had a special flavor for the young teacher, for it had the stillness of the forest, broken only by the occasional lonely notes of birdsong. The peaceful silence always soothed him, and today his ruffled temper needed soothing. He sat down on a fallen log under the friendly cedar tree and cradled his chin in his hands.

Bitterness welled up in him as he thought of the injustice of the farmer's demand. He now understood the impotent frustration of the falsely accused. Not a person he had seen since he returned from that miserable trip had shown any compassion—or even friendliness. Was it because he was a stranger? Or was it their way of telling him to "go back where you come from?"

Laurence thought back over his summer's work and then glanced down at the holes in his shoes. Perhaps he should leave. He had nothing to show yet for all his efforts. Nothing, that is, except the memory of an occasional flicker of hope in a blank dark eye. But was that enough to keep him going? He had no money nor hope of any. And now they all seemed bent on freezing him out. . . .

So far his crop of ideas had reaped little more than discomfort— and trouble. What was it Aunt Liza used to say about trouble? "Trouble is so high you can't climb over it, so wide you can't walk 'round it, so deep you can't dig under it, so I be doggoned iffen de only way to beat it ain't to duck yo' haid and *wade right through!*"

As his temper cooled in the peaceful stillness of the forest, Laurence realized he could not leave with a bad debt hanging over him, even though he felt it unjustified. Not only for the sake of his own pride, but for the faith of these woods people. They had scant reason to trust a stranger, and this would feed their latent suspicions. This would prove the ones who had no faith in him had been right. Besides, he should have paid attention and seen to it that the boy took care of that horse. That was the price of pre-occupation.

The only thing to do, Laurence decided with a sigh, was "duck" his head and "wade right through." After all, that was what Walter Scott and Mark Twain had both done when confronted with debts with which their names were connected even though they had not been legally responsible.

Laurence quickly rose from the log, his mind clear. Leaving was not the question. But about the horse there was only one answer. He must take the responsibility. On the other hand, that did not mean playing the fool. The $175 that the man asked was exorbitant.

Laurence told Amon his intentions of paying for the animal but asked that a meeting be called so that members of the community could decide on a fair price.

Amon nodded his approval. "You is doin' right," he said.

When the meeting was held, Amon spoke for Laurence and another man for the owner of the horse. After hearing both sides, the group decided that $125 would be a fair price.

Privately, Laurence felt that $25 would have been fairer, but he did not quibble. His problem now was where to get the money.

"Do you want to borrow the money?" someone asked.

Laurence looked up quickly, saw a cold-eyed man with high cheekbones who stood on the outside of the little knot of men.

"I'll loan it to you on time."

Laurence realized that this was Ed Taylor, the only colored man in the community who had any cash. He met Taylor's shrewd, cold glance and found nothing frightening in it. It was the same thing he had seen in the faces of many men who knew how to make a profit in any business. "Yes," he said, "I'd like to borrow the money—if you can give me a reasonable rate of interest and enough time."

"A year," said Taylor, "at 10 per cent."

Laurence reached out his hand. "Fair enough," he said.

"Meet you at my house tomorrow," said Taylor, "and give you a check after we draw up the papers."

"I'll be there," Laurence said.

As Taylor strode away, Amon sighed. "Don't know as Ah'd a-done that if I was you," he said softly.

"There was nothing else to do."

The farmer whose horse had died came up to Laurence and said, "I jes' hope Uncle Ed don't skin you fer it."

"I don't think he will," Laurence said. "It was a fair deal. I'll bring the money to your farm tomorrow."

The farmer thanked him and went on his way. As Laurence started to leave, he found that he was suddenly the center of eager attention. Most of the men, instead of going their own way, walked along by his side, clasping his arm with warm, friendly hands and congratulating him.

"Yo's a good man, 'Fesser, to take it like that," one of them said.

"That was mighty fine—agreein' to pay for that horse."

One man whispered in his ear, "Pus'nly, I thought you was cha'ged too much."

At supper that night Amon said earnestly, "It was jus' right for you to take low, 'Fesser. They'll all be for you 'roun' hyear from now on."

"Take low!"

Laurence understood. He had assumed more than he was actually responsible for. He had "taken low" to the horse owner, even though he felt the charge unjust. It was a position that southern colored people well understood, for it was a position that they took daily in reference to the whites. For this reason they reacted with sympathy and personal identification to the man who did the same. He was a man who bore the burden of guilt, of accusation for a false charge with dignity, without fighting back.

Again he thought of one of Aunt Liza's garbled versions of biblical advice: "When somebody fetch you a clip on one o' yo' cheeks, turn de other one, an' ef he fetch you a clip on dat one, den de Lawd be wid de righteous."

Everywhere Laurence went among the colored people from that day forward he was greeted with respect and with an inclusive friendliness. He had proved himself on the side of the meek.

Chapter 5

"He Ain't No Fool"

It was refreshing for Laurence suddenly to find himself a respected member of the community, but it still had not built a school
for him. Twice more he made futile attempts to plead his cause at
religious conventions—once at the special invitation of the meeting's president, only to receive the same interlocking cold shoulder.
The various leaders of the impoverished communities, jealous of
what little power they had and what meager funds they were able to
enlist for their own causes, had no use for the young "furriner."
Despite these rebuffs on the leader level, however, Laurence still
stubbornly clung to the belief that there was a powerful host gradually coming over on his side—the farm wives with their eight, ten,
and twelve children who listened so intently when he spoke of
school, the farmers who would nod their heads, muttering "dat's
right" as he talked of the necessity for other crops than cotton.

They were there waiting and hoping, Laurence felt, just as he had
sensed it that first night at the Christmas frolic, and he had looked
into the faces lighted by the pine-knot fire, who, despite their
jostling gaiety of the moment before, had listened quietly as he
spoke of another kind of Christmas and another way of living.

But how to reach them? For that the young teacher had no
answer. He knew they would help him, these country folk, if
"agonizin' in prayer" would help, or "totin' a load of wood."

As he had done so many times that apparently fruitless season
Laurence went one morning to the log under the great cedar tree to
analyze, to figure, and to plan. Surely there was an answer somewhere.

When he left the Gibson farmhouse he took with him his day's
mail that he had picked up that morning at Braxton—some farm

pamphlets from Iowa, newspapers, a magazine, letters from home. He had not as yet received a reply to the letters he had sent out asking for funds although plenty of time had elapsed. As he made his way through the cedar brake into the little clearing, he got a cool drink from the spring, then sat down on his log and tried to think.

Around him the warm red earth was curtained by a blue sky, over him the lofty branches of the ancient trees spread their shade, before him the old sheep shed loomed picturesquely from among tall weeds.

Yes, somewhere lay the answer. He never came to this spot but that he felt a message of hope. But where was the key?

Then, suddenly, Laurence realized he was not alone. He looked up to see a half-grown barefoot boy standing, like a heron poised for flight, at the edge of the clearing, balanced between strong curiosity and equally strong timidity.

"Hello." Laurence nodded to the boy, pointed to the log beside him. "Come sit down." He recognized the youngster as coming from a nearby farm.

A quick, shy grin relaxed the boy's features and he took a seat at the other end of the log.

Absently Laurence handed him one of his newspapers, began thumbing through his magazine, then, suddenly, he stared at his visitor.

The boy had accepted the proffered newspaper and was now holding it in front of him, examining it with minute animal curiosity. The paper was upside down.

Laurence looked from the paper to the blank dark eyes that gazed uncomprehendingly at the column of words.

"Aren't you going to read it?" he asked.

"Nassuh." The boy looked up with a quick sheepish grin. "Ah cain't read."

Laurence studied the youth a moment—the gangling youth with his sturdy bare feet, tattered overalls, and wide, guileless eyes. "How old are you?"

"Goin' on sixteen."

"Would you *like* to know how to read?" Laurence asked.

The boy's eyes flashed in a burst of ecstasy. "Oh, yassuh, 'Fesser," he said, "I sho'ly would!"

"Well, come back tomorrow—this same time," Laurence said, "and I'll start teaching you."

"Oh, thank you, thank you, 'Fesser." The boy rose from the log, his big toes wriggling in the grass in excitement. "I'll be hyear." Off he tore down the dusty trail.

Laurence smiled as he watched the boy's loose-jointed loping figure disappear down the path.

Well, he had a school! One student, anyhow. Laurence felt an odd relief as he considered his spontaneous act. What was it they had said about Mark Hopkins on one end of a log and a student on the other constituting a school? Well, it looked like the historical process was about to be repeated.

He was broke, he was in debt, and he had not as yet begun to raise a fund for a school building. So far as his plans went, he certainly was at the bottom. Therefore—Laurence chuckled aloud with a boyish lift of confidence—there was obviously nowhere to go but up!

The next morning, when the young teacher came to his log, he found waiting for him his first student plus two friends of about the same age and background. The three boys were all farm born and bred and not one of them could read. They knew nothing about farming except to plant, hoe, and pick cotton, and yet they must make their living off a farm. They could not figure, so they had no way of knowing what they would or should get for their labor or their crops, nor whether they received what they were supposed to.

Laurence greeted his class, then stood before them. We shall begin by singing 'Praise God from Whom All Blessings Flow.' "

As the three young voices rose on the still forest air, blending with their teacher's in the joyous hymn, Laurence sensed that the woods had come alive. To one side he more felt than saw a pair of eyes in a thicket, and as soon as the hymn was ended, he called out in a cheery voice, "Come and join us."

The bushes parted slowly and a bent figure crept cautiously out of the covering of the deep brush and stood hesitantly before them. It was an old man of undetermined vintage, whose twisted grotesque legs, wrapped in strips of burlap sacking, were aided by a cane. His body was covered with dirty tatters of unrecognizable clothing, and a big ivory comb was stuck rakishly over one ear in the long bushy hair. A felt derby-like hat rested on the back of his grizzled head and over his shoulder he carried a Civil War musket.

"Good morning, sir," Laurence called. "We're about to begin class. Would you like to join us?"

"D-d-d-don' ca' if Ah does," said the old man, as he took a seat on the end of the log.

"Mornin', Uncle Tom," one of the boys said. Then turning to the teacher, he added, "This is Uncle Tom Brown, he lives back yander." He jerked his thumb toward the deep woods.

"Do you live alone?" Laurence asked, a question more out of curiosity than politeness because the spot indicated was in the deepest and densest part of the woods.

"N-n-n-nah, suh, n-n-n-nah, suh." The old man bared his gums in a wide, friendly grin. "Ah d-d-d-don' live alone. Me an-nn de Lawd lives dere."

"Oh!" said Laurence, feeling somehow put in his place. "Let's begin with a Bible lesson." He took out his pocket Bible and started to read, and as he did so, he again had the feeling that the woods were again "coming alive."

Less bashful than Uncle Tom, the local farmers began drifting in, some of them bringing boys, and took seats on the log until it was full, then the rest of them squatted on the ground. Word had passed with the swift mouth-to-mouth communication of a country community that today the 'fesser was going to teach a boy how to "read and write." It was something they all had "a min' to learn if it wasn't too late."

By the time he had finished the opening Bible lesson, Laurence had a class of twelve—five boys and seven men. Among the men was his old friend Amon, who announced he was not "jinin' " but that he would "come 'roun' and lissen" whenever he had time off from his farm work. There was Hector McLaurin, a substantial, hardworking young farmer who asked, " 'Fesser, do you think Ah could learn to read and write 'fo' plantin' time in de spring?" There was young William Dixon at whose parents' house Laurence had frequently found a warm welcome. Then there was William Yancy whose father and grandfather had been carpenters, and who had the advantage of a little schooling and knew a trade as well.

Bible lessons and spirituals, Laurence had already found, were the older men's "meat." In lives relatively devoid of pleasure they had always found solace in their Bibles. Even those who could not read a word could quote scripture on endless scripture which they had learned "by ear" in church. They "sang out" the old slave songs of faith, endurance, and hope with harmonious sincerity till the woods rang with their strong voices.

Religion was an everyday part of all their lives. And Laurence made up his mind, that first day, that it would always be a part of his school. Not one man's religion or another's, but all men's religions—a simple no-creed devotion to the teachings of Christ.

Bible teaching over, Laurence began his first lesson in how to read.

At the sawmill Miss Nannie could hardly wait to spread the news. "Mr. Webster," she burst out as her tall boss appeared in the office door, "do you know what that crazy Jones has done? He's gone and started a school right out in the woods under that cedar tree on the old Mordecai Harris place."

John Webster looked down at his secretary, his eyes growing thoughtful as he looked through and beyond her. "Jones may be crazy," he mused, "but he ain't no fool!"

As his thoughts fell into the words of the popular song of that time, Miss Nannie and Albert laughed in delight. From then on the sawmill people and their neighbors spoke of the young teacher who had settled so strangely in their midst with the appellation, "He may be crazy but he ain't no fool!"

Though he had started his school on a moment's whim, with no backing, building, or equipment of any kind, Laurence saw to it that what he was doing became known to the community so that people would realize there was nothing to fear in the little group that assembled each day in the woods. He sent word, to both white and colored, that visitors were welcome. The curious who came found the proceedings innocent enough to squelch whatever suspicions they might have had.

Each morning Laurence proceeded with his first-day schedule: school opened with a hymn, progressed from that to scripture lessons, then "readin' and writin'" followed. As soon as his students were far enough along to participate, he began holding spelling matches at the end of each class to impress the words on their memories as well as to provide a form of amusement.

As his group enlarged, Laurence enlisted the services of Yancy and Dixon, both of whom had had a little schooling. This both helped him out and stimulated their interest. They were his first faculty.

By the time the first cool October winds blew across the Piney Woods Laurence had thirty students ranging in ages from seven to sixty. To keep warm some of the students chopped wood and kept a brisk fire going close to where the classes met in a huddle, then they took their turn learning while the others chopped wood.

He might not have a school in the strict physical sense of a plant and equipment, Laurence decided, but if a school meant a bunch of eager students and a teacher, this little group in the clearing at Piney Woods more than qualified.

November found half a hundred students sitting on logs rolled up close to the bonfire. To further keep warm, in addition to chopping wood for the fire, under Yancy's direction some of them worked on hand-hewn rough benches which could eventually replace the logs.

It was just a question of time, however, when the weather would force them inside or compel them to quit. Laurence had long had his eye on the deserted sheep shed. Though originally a cabin, the old building was now little more than a rough shell in which lambs, lizards, snakes, and owls sought shelter. Tall weeds hid all but the roof from view. But, figured Laurence, as he moved from class to class across the clearing, any shelter was better than none. After class one morning he and Yancy cut down enough of the dry weeds to get a look at the walls and roof.

"It could be fixed up, I reckon," was the carpenter's verdict. "Run down, but the foundation's pretty sturdy."

That evening Laurence asked Amon who owned the place.

"Uncle Ed Taylor got it on a bad debt," Amon said. "Too po' to sprout cowpeas or it'd be planted."

Uncle Ed! Laurence swallowed. "I was figuring on fixing up that old sheep shed to hold school in"—Laurence was more thinking out loud than talking—"if he would let us have it."

"He won't let you have it if he knows you want it," snorted Amon, "even if he hasn't no mo' use for it than a hog with a sidesaddle. I tell you, 'Fesser, old Uncle Ed's mean!"

"Well"—Laurence shrugged his shoulders—"there is no harm in trying."

Amon stared at him. "You mean you got the nerve to ask?"

"He can't do more than pitch me out."

"I've prayed fo' you befo' dis, 'Fesser," Amon said, shaking his head, "but now I'm goin' to put my min' to it!"

As he headed up the path that led to the Taylor cabin Laurence made out the figure of a man plowing with a mule in a field behind the house. He headed for the field and when he got within earshot called out.

Ed Taylor turned to peer at his visitor, nodded shortly, and went on plowing.

Laurence called to him again. Taylor went right on with his work, seemingly oblivious to his visitor's desire to talk. Laurence leaned down, rolled up his trousers legs, and plodded out into the newly plowed field. He got into the row parallel to Uncle Ed—the plowed one that was free of cotton stalks—so that he could walk abreast.

" 'Evening," said Laurence.

Uncle Ed peered at him, his shrewd eyes narrow over his high cheekbones. "Evenin'," he grunted, and returned his attention to his mule.

"Got something I want to talk to you about," Laurence shouted.

"Yap," said Uncle Ed, making his turn and starting another row. Laurence turned back in the furrow the farmer had just finished.

"I've started a school," he said.

"So I heard," said Uncle Ed.

"—on your land," Laurence finished bravely.

"Yap, I heard," said Uncle Ed.

"I've got a favor to ask of you," Laurence said as Ed popped his whip.

"So's eve'body else," shouted Uncle Ed, doggedly keeping on with his plowing, actually making his mule move faster.

"You remember that old sheep shed," called Laurence, now in a slow trot to keep up.

"Co'se," said Uncle Ed.

"Mind if I fix it up and take my class inside for the winter months?"

"We'll see." Taylor peered up at the darkening sky, pulled his mule to a halt, and began unhitching it from the plow. "I'll take out and talk to you, now it's dark," he said.

Laurence padded behind while Uncle Ed led the mule into the barn lot, turned him loose, fed him, then headed for the house.

At the door Laurence hesitated. It was suppertime, and he could see a woman's figure bending over the fireplace inside.

"Come in and eat," said Uncle Ed.

"Thank you." Laurence followed the spare, grim-faced older man into the house.

Over a silent supper, served to the two men by Taylor's taciturn wife, Laurence studied the man before him. Looking at the sharp, intelligent eyes, the spare, tight-skinned face, he realized this was a different type of colored man from the illiterate, easy-going, and loquacious farmers he had heretofore met in the Piney Woods country.

"Now," Taylor wiped the last bite of beans from his plate with a bit of corn bread, swallowed it, leaned back, and pulled out his pipe, "tell me what you're up to."

Realizing that he at last had his host's attention, Laurence briefly went over his idea for a school, told what he had done that summer, and how, seemingly, he had failed until he had accidentally started the school on the log. He particularly emphasized his disappointment in not enlisting the help of the various church associations.

"There's no he'p there," Taylor said. "Pahsons all too jealous of each other. I could have told you that."

"But I wanted to get everyone behind me in faith if not in money," Laurence explained, "colored and whites both. I figured that was the only chance I had to start a school and keep it going."

"What are you teachin' 'em?" Taylor asked, his shrewd eyes boring into the young man's.

"How to read and write at the moment," Laurence said, "but after that I want to get into trades—how to make brooms, shoe horses, raise stock, can fruit, keep house. . . ."

"You intend to take girls, too, then?"

"Yes, indeed. Women have as much to do with raising the general standard of living as the men. They should learn how best to care for their kitchens, chicken yards, and vegetable patches. They should learn how to sew properly, how to plan a proper diet and prepare it, how to do a good job of housework whether at home or if they work out."

"Yes, yes," mused Taylor. "I saw a woman trying to cut out a dress with a butcher knife the other day and another one feeding her child alum for a snakebite—wonder it didn't die."

"I'm not concerned with what they call 'book larnin'," Laurence went on eagerly, happy to talk to a man who could follow what he said. "What I want to overcome is basic ignorance and superstition. Just give them a chance at life so they can take pride in their work, keep up their houses better, eat better, save a little money . . ."

". . . and give their children a fighting chance," finished Taylor, his eyes mellowing, perhaps with a private dream of his own. Then, suddenly, the haze vanished and he focused his bright eyes once again upon the young teacher. "I was a slave once. I got out—by accident—and after the war went North, where I got a little education. I was able to get a job and make some money. Then I came back here and put what I had saved in land." He looked at Laurence a long, sad moment. "Do you realize I'm probably one of the three or four colored men in this whole country who owns anything? Most of them share crop these little old chunks of land, or rent it. Hasn't even occurred to them to try to save up and buy their own strip. In the first place, they've never got over five cents ahead in their lives— except at Christmas!" Taylor was silent another moment, his eyes once more occupied with inner thoughts. "They think I'm hard— and mean," he said slowly, "because I work my land and make money and tend to my own business. The difference between me and the rest of them is I've seen something, I've seen what the world can be like beyond these poor hills."

Laurence started to speak, then something held him back as he watched the expression on Taylor's proud, cold face.

Suddenly Taylor rose from the table with a brisk movement, clapped the younger man's shoulder with his heavy farmer's hand, and his face softened.

"Tell you what I'll do," he said. "I'll give you that old sheep shed if you think you can do anything with it, and the forty acres around it where you're teaching now."

"Thank you, Mr. Taylor," Laurence cried, his hand outstretched in gratitude. Taylor ignored it.

". . . and $50," he continued. "By the looks of you, you could use it for food if not for the school."

Laurence lowered his eyes in embarrassment. It was true. He had had plenty of reason to think about the Piney Woods story about the man who ate dried peas for breakfast, water for lunch, and swelled up for supper. Whether he had eaten or not in the past months had depended upon the invitations he had received along toward mealtime. And even then not much, because he had hated to take it from the limited amount that most families had. But of all people it surprised him that it was Uncle Ed Taylor who noticed how thin he was getting.

"I don't know how to thank you," Laurence said, his voice low with sincerity.

"All I want you to do is make it work," said Taylor. "That will be thanks enough. Here's the fifty." He went to a dresser drawer, unlocked an iron box, took out fifty one-dollar bills, and gave them to Laurence. "This has nothing to do with the $125 you owe me. We'll get to that next year. I'll fix up a deed for the forty acres. How do you want it made out?"

"To the Piney Woods Country Life School," Laurence said impulsively.

Uncle Ed smiled. "I think it might be a good idea if you wait till a Sunday to tell folks," he said with a sly grin. "Might stir up some to do likewise."

Laurence smiled joyfully. "I think we're about to go into a partnership," he said.

"You're right," said Uncle Ed. "This is something I believe in. I'll help you all I can."

When Laurence headed down the road toward Amon Gibson's farm he shook his head in amazement. So this was "cold, hard-hearted Ed Taylor." You surely never knew where good luck was coming from or what it would look like when it appeared. This should be a lesson. He had gone to Taylor out of desperation, and he had received the most tangible help and expression of confidence that had come so far.

Laurence gazed up at the benevolent orange November moon and let out a whoop of joy. This was his happiest moment since he had left college.

Chapter 6

"It's Mo' Dan a Mystery"

It was perhaps the hardest thing Laurence had ever done—to keep that secret. He wanted to go forth singing it to the skies. But he sensed the value of the shrewd old man's advice. There was to be a big meeting a couple of Sundays off and he secured Uncle Ed's promise to be there and also a promise from the preacher to let him make an announcement to the congregation.

When he entered the little church building and took his seat up front, he glanced around and, true to his promise, there was Uncle Ed back in a corner almost out of sight.

A couple of spirituals were sung, one of the brethren prayed, then the preacher went to the pulpit.

"Ladies and gen'men," he began, "I wants you, befo' I preach, to listen to de noble words of one of de most notorious men of our community, a man who, though young in years and in face, has proved to our doubtin' eyes that he knows de unknowable, thinks de unthinkable, an' kin unscrew de unscrutable! Ladies and gen'men, I deduces you to 'Fesser Jones."

The preacher bowed to Laurence and with a sweeping gesture indicated that he was to take his place behind the pulpit. A little startled, Laurence mumbled out his thanks, went to the pulpit, and faced the crowd.

"As you all know," he began in his clear, earnest voice, "I have started a little school down here in the woods. It was begun without support, without money, without even a roof over us. But I think as of today things are going to be different. Just the past few days we have received the first major contribution to the school." He took from his pocket both the deed to the land and the cabin and the money Uncle Ed had given him and held them up. "I want to announce to you all that Uncle Ed Taylor has generously donated

53

not only the forty acres on the old Mordecai Harris place and the cabin on it but also $50 toward the erection of a building in which to house our classes."

There was a light applause, an undercurrent of whispered words, and then one of the deacons in the church sprang to his feet.

"It's a trick," he shouted. "I ain't a-goin' to have nothin' to do with it. If Ed Taylor give you dat land and money there's a trick to it somewheres. Taylor ain't done dat if there ain't a trick to it."

Laurence's face flushed. "I think you should apologize," he said sharply. "This gift came out of generosity and understanding. It's for all of us, and I won't stand to hear you talk that way about it."

"Don't pay him no mind," a deep voice boomed out. Laurence saw Uncle Ed on his feet in the back of the room. He motioned for Laurence to keep quiet. "He's got his reasons for thinking that way," Taylor went on, his shrewd glance sweeping the room. "Folks here haven't seen me spreading my money around much to help anybody else. Reason is, I haven't seen any use in it up to now." His glance again swept the church and came to rest on the deacon, who tried to duck out of sight. Uncle Ed smiled. "Folks aren't even used to seeing me here in church," he went on. "Mrs. Taylor comes, but I haven't even felt like supportin' the church. There was too much to be done and too little to do it with. But here"—Uncle Ed clenched one hard fist, smacked it into the palm of his other hand— "here now we got something we can all work on, something real that's already happening. It's not a dream off somewheres. We didn't like the 'Fesser when he first come here, figgerin' he was just another furriner full of big talk and big promises, but he's proved now that isn't so. We didn't help him, so he went right ahead and started a school in spite of us. That's enough for me. From now on I'm aimin' to help all I can. I've put up that $50 to show how I feel about it, and there ain't no trick to it. I believe in this Jones and I want the rest of you to believe in him, too. He's proved himself without no help from any of us."

A spontaneous burst of applause rocked the room, interspersed with "amens," and anything more that Ed Taylor had to say was lost in the excitement. Laurence could not have spoken if he had wanted to. The lump in his throat was the size of a turnip.

The deacon who had spoken out against Ed Taylor rose and, as the noise subsided, said, "I think Brother Taylor's proved to us all jus' why he done what he done." Then he sat down.

"He sho'ly has, he sho'ly has," cried out an old woman, rocking her body in rhythm to her words.

A small, calm-browed farmer rose from his bench. "I think mebbe I could see mah way to give fifteen dollars," he said. It was Hector McLaurin who had come to the cedar log to learn to read and write.

Amon Gibson stood up next. "Been too bad a crop year for me to give any money to help 'Fesser Jones with," he said, "but I got that pair a' gray mules and a wagon that I'd be proud to loan 'em when they got haulin' to do."

"Thank you, Amon," Laurence said quietly.

On and on it went. All sorts of things, including small sums of money, were offered. Somehow the thing was taking shape before his eyes—a real school, with a real building. It was not so much the promise of physical help but the spirit that counted. Heretofore Laurence had been able only to bring a flicker of hope to tired, work-worn eyes. But today there was more than hope—there was an atmosphere of real belief that what they had felt was a vague dream —like freedom and justice on earth—was now a living, earthly possibility within their grasp—something that all of them might see come to pass within their own lifetime and not in that dim "tomorrow" for which they mostly lived. As he thought these things, there was another voice:

"I ain't got no money, nor no mules either," a man was saying as he twisted his battered hat in nervous hands, "but I sho' will he'p rive out de boa'ds when you sta't buildin' yo' schoolhouse."

"Rive out de boa'ds!" Laurence's answering smile was just as warm as if he had known what the man meant, for he realized that it meant work and that it came from a heart that knew no doubts.

A thin, spare figure in calico rose and stepped out into the aisle. "When you git you some lumbah and git sta'ted building," she said, "us womenfolks will bring in food and he'p in dat way."

"Indeed you can." Laurence went down the aisle, pressed her hand gratefully, then spoke from there. "I want to thank you all from the bottom of my heart. Your response gives me the courage to go on. I'm going to call a meeting for next Saturday—I want you all to be there. I'm going to ask everyone who will come—white and colored

—from Braxton, from all over Simpson and Rankin counties. Bring what you have promised, and tell your neighbors and friends. With your help, and God's help, I think that by the time the sun goes down we'll have the beginnings of a real school for our children."

The next morning, after classes, now free of the secrecy under which Uncle Ed had placed him, Laurence put his students to work under Yancy's direction to get the sheep shed ready as a temporary classroom. This would be their first lesson in work-your-way plan for student labor in exchange for learning. They were to clear away the weeds, brace the roof, put in a new floor, build a dirt-and-stick chimney, rechink between the logs, and then whitewash the building inside and out. When he had them busily at work, he started for Comby and Webster's sawmill.

When Laurence entered the office of the sawmill one glance told the sawmill owner that this was no ordinary visit.

"What do you want today, Jones?" Webster asked.

"Help."

Laurence then told Webster what had happened and of his need for lumber with which to build.

"But what if you do get a building up," Webster asked, "then what? You don't have any state aid. How do you expect to keep a school going? Your pupils aren't going to be able to pay anything. Where is the money coming from?"

"I have friends up North," Laurence said, "people I went to school with and whom I know intimately. I feel that they will support a school like this."

"Have you gotten anything from them yet?"

Laurence flushed. "No," he admitted, "I have not."

"Yet you have asked them?" Webster persisted.

"Yes, I have." Laurence's head came up. "But I haven't had anything to show yet. They're not willing to put any money in me till I have something to show."

"You think they will then?" asked Webster.

"I'm sure they will," said Laurence. "I know they will—when I have a building up and a school going, and can write and tell them about it, send them pictures, give them a day-by-day progress about what is happening. I know they'll help."

"They had better," Webster said grimly, "for you won't get any money out of here."

A feeling of desperation came over Laurence. Did this mean that Webster would not help? Was this the end of the interview? He saw Webster turn his head away and blow softly on the point of a pencil he held between his fingers.

"What are you teaching?" Webster suddenly asked, his eyes now focused sharply on Laurence's face.

"I would be glad for you to come see, Mr. Webster," he said. "We're starting with elementary reading and writing on the premise that they are the key to everything else. Then we are going to teach trades, farming, caring for animals and equipment, cooking, sewing, better work habits."

"You think you can make better workers out of the niggers?"

"That is what I hope to do," Laurence said. "To make better farmers, teach them how to be more saving, and eventually to bring to them a higher standard of living. When we get a bigger building up, I can start more classes. I already have one student who can teach carpentry."

"Tell you what I'll do." Webster wheeled around, yanked open his desk drawer. "I'll give you ten thousand feet of lumber to start with and all the rest you want on credit." He drew out an order blank and started writing.

The office air was tense as Webster's pen scratched. Miss Nannie and Albert sat as if frozen, with their mouths open, awaiting the big thank-you speech that would follow. Instead, Laurence took the order, pocketed it, stared keenly at the big man's kind eyes. "All I hope is, Mr. Webster," he said softly, "that what I do makes you glad, and proud, that you did this for me." With a swift bow he was gone.

Miss Nannie and Albert stared at each other, then over at their boss.

"Well, I never!" exploded Miss Nannie.

"Imagine," said Albert. "He pulled your leg for ten thousand feet of lumber and not even a thank-you speech!"

John Webster looked at his employees, then at the door through which Laurence had gone. "He said enough," Webster said, and went back to work.

That evening, as Laurence sat with Amon Gibson before the fire-place, Amon said softly, " 'Fesser, it's mo' dan a mystery, as de song say, it's a miracle."

Chapter 7

The Pure in Heart

It was a happy day for Laurence when he and Yancy moved into the old sheep shed, now converted into living quarters and a temporary classroom. This meant that they were right on the grounds to keep things going. A few days later four more boys, who came from so far away that they lost most of their time coming and going from home, also moved in with them. With John Webster's lumber and Uncle Ed's $50 Laurence hoped the coming Saturday meeting would add enough in the way of money, supplies, and man power to provide the minimum needs. It had been obvious from the beginning that only a boarding school could offer any continuity of education in such a scattered community. Besides that, the visual evidence of a building erected solely for student housing and education would both whip up and keep up the interest of the local people and serve as tangible evidence to his northern friends that he had been able to put his educational theories into actual operation.

Familiar as he now was with the curiosity and love of excitement that drew backwoods communities into ready cluster, Laurence was not prepared for the masses of humanity that began pouring into the little clearing even before the appointed hour. Afoot, clogging the rutted trails and footpaths through the woods, on horseback and muleback, some in farm wagons and oxcarts, the country folks— work-worn parents and stair-stepped broods of children—poured from the thickets and from the woods like ants from a log on fire. Sprinkled among them were quite a few whites, including John Webster and Wiley Mangum. Laurence's ready helpers, anxious to show off what they had learned, counted more than eleven hundred.

When he finally managed to get the crowd quiet, after telling them about John Webster's and Ed Taylor's generous gifts, Laurence called upon a number of his present brood of fifty students to get up and tell what they were learning. Surprisingly, they did it without fear, their glowing eyes helping to carry the message of what they were going to be able to take home with them in what they had learned, to be of more value to their parents, their communities, and themselves.

Laurence then outlined to the crowd what he had not dared to do before, his program for a full-scale boarding school to which students could come from far-off communities and stay a full term, working out their tuition and board, or paying part and working the rest. He pointed out the need for an education of this sort in terms that both white and colored could understand. Carefully, step by step, he explained how, starting at this "bottom rail" of humanity, the standards of living could be built up that, in turn, would raise the level of the community and make money and therefore a better living for the merchant, the banker, and the sawmill owner.

As Laurence spoke, he took note of the reaction of what he said on John Webster, and knew from the expression on Webster's face that it met with his approval.

This was particularly important at the time. With the shadow of Governor Vardeman, who had just abolished the only Negro normal school in the state with the explanation that "Negro education is a threat to white supremacy," dulling the Mississippi landscape, Laurence had to watch his step. "Here we ask for nothing more than a chance at practical training, religious instruction, and ordinary human rights," he said. "We want to teach our boys and girls how to work with their hands so they will be able to make a living; teach them enough reading and writing so they can say what is on their minds; and give them moral and religious training as a substitute for superstition and fear."

He then told them that it was a part of their responsibility and duty to help build the building in which this could take place. "Mr. Webster has given us ten thousand feet of lumber for our building; Uncle Ed Taylor, in addition to this land, has given $50 to buy additional materials; Hector McLaurin has contributed $15; Amon Gibson has loaned us his wagon and mule team. Now, I ask all of you, if you believe in this school and want to see it materialize before your eyes, to give what you can."

As Laurence stood there people began to come forward, the white men with their bills, the colored with their quarters, dimes, nickels, and even pennies—pennies which meant the difference between an extra bag of meal to last the month out. One farmer promised half a hog when he butchered, another a third of the proceeds of his one bale of cotton that he had salvaged from the boll weevils and the rain.

Suddenly Laurence saw a wave of people draw back and a lone figure walk slowly forward, a tall, thin figure of a woman who walked with a strange dignity. An old country woman, slim and tall, her cotton dress faded from many washings, the cracks of her shoes red with trail dirt of the four miles she had walked that day, and her head high under a flopping sunbonnet. Before her she led, as some ancient ebony princess might have led a brace of hunting hounds, two live geese on a string.

" 'Fesser," said the woman in a rich country voice, "I'se a widder woman, and this is all I'se got to give. But I'se got nine chillun, and I sho' wants dis school to go up!"

Fifty dollars and a brace of geese; ten thousand feet of lumber and half a hog; a hundred and nineteen pennies and a jug of sorghum; a thousand black faces lighted with an eager hope and the will to work—such was the spirit in which the Piney Woods Country Life School began its physical growth.

There were prayers of thanksgiving, a few rousing spirituals, and finally an hour set to begin work the following Monday morning, then the enthusiastic congregation dispersed, taking up the trail, by mule, team, or foot, to their meager homes with a dream for their children lighting their eyes.

The spirit of the Saturday meeting had caught and held. First the men appeared, as they had promised, with their saws, their hammers, their axes, their nails, their mules, ready to work. And what was important, Laurence noticed with a glow of inner satisfaction, they appeared *on time*. A sense of time was something that they needed to learn.

Before beginning work Laurence, boyish and slender in a new pair of overalls, led the group in prayer, a lesson from the Scriptures, and then a joyous spiritual.

They fell to work with a will, with a vigor that belied all that Laurence had heard about their industry. Here was the clue. Give them a job they believed in and they would not only be punctual but work with a hearty enjoyment. No doubt the long, deadening slave years, with no incentive for a job well done, had stripped most of them and their children of their pride in good work.

Laurence, his student years still close enough to feel the symbolism and import of the occasion, joined the men at the crosscut saw as they felled the first tree.

All morning long the group of untrained and unskilled but willing volunteer builders labored at their job under Yancy's direction—hauling lumber, readying the ground, preparing the foundation, swinging axes, or whatever job needed to be done.

At noon the women began to appear, sturdy farmers' wives, trudging with their laden baskets over the hills and pastures, up the rutted trails from their homes to the school grounds "carryin' the food," their eyes shielded from the noon glare by flapping cotton sunbonnets and with great aprons tenting their waists.

Mounds of baked sweet potatoes, pots of still-warm cow- and black-eyed peas cooked with a snippet of precious sowbelly, blackened skillets of corn bread, jugs of buttermilk, pans of greens—collard and turnips and kale that had mellowed long, lazy hours on the back of wood stoves—all this was brought to give more energy for more work. And then to top it off, "tater" pies—brown flaky crusts and rich sweet-potato fillings sweetened with homemade molasses.

A sumptuous feast for tired workers—one for which they could give thanks, in low-voiced prayer, before they sat down under the shade of the trees, eating and resting till they were again ready to go back to work.

Laurence used this rest dinner hour to lecture on farming, then he called on the various individuals to tell their experiences, after which the group analyzed them. Grouped together in a common project, with hope before them and neighbors at their side rather than in lonely isolation of their day-to-day life, it was easier for them to grasp the simple truth that the failure of a corn crop might have been caused by bad seed than because some enemy had brought it about by putting a "jack" or "tobus" powder on their doorsteps in a fit of anger. Also Laurence sought a careful balance between scientific truth and their beliefs, whether religious or purely superstitious, so that he would not disturb them too violently. It was, he said, quite proper to call upon God for His help, but not to blame Fate with something that was really the product of ignorance and superstition.

"Pray as if it all depended on God," he advised, *"but work as if it all depended on you!"*

After the other workers had gone home Laurence and Yancy continued on until darkness forced them to quit. Then they went to the cabin, ate a cold supper, and fell wearily on their cots to sleep until the first streaks of dawn awakened them.

Day followed day with the same pattern. The workers continued to come, the women were there every day with the food, then another "short lesson" in farming, and back to work till "fust dark." With this kind of persistence the building mushroomed.

Then came the tornado.

Straight up from the Gulf, tearing across soft, defenseless farm land, uprooting huge trees, smashing houses, killing livestock, leaving a trail of death and destruction.

As Laurence and Yancy lay on their cots in the corner of the little old sheep shed, praying for their very lives, they could hear the snap and crash of forest pines and cedars, the sickening crunch of giant trees as they came to the ground, the crescendo of mighty thunder, the howl and roar and fury of vicious wind. Flashes of lightning fired the cabin with a blaze of unearthly light, only to disappear and leave the impenetrable blackness of the storm. The shudder and creak and agonizing cries of the old logs of their cabin, as they feebly resisted the strain of the wind, the scrunching groan as a tree limb lashed across the old roof, constantly reminded them that they might be out in the storm at any moment.

A night of terror, then the strange sudden silence of morning when the "bad child" nature has exhausted her naughtiest mood and suddenly turns an innocent, clean face, with a pallid sun smiling through the last of the drifting, now-impotent clouds.

Laurence and Yancy got up from their cots, their muscles still taut from the burden of tension and fear, and as they looked around marveled that they were alive. Somehow the fifty-year-old cabin had snugged down to the earth, settled creakily against solid ground, and hung on. When they tried to go outside they wondered that this had been so. Their roof, windows, and the door itself were blocked by piled-up limbs and even whole trees. They managed to climb over the wreckage and made their way into the clearing toward the new building.

One look and Laurence felt the quick tears of childhood scald his eyes and tighten his throat. The building had not actually blown over, but it had been lifted from its foundation and twisted into a grotesque shape. The top had been blown out of the ancient cedar under which he had held his first classes. Only the trunk with a few ragged branches at the top had withstood the force of the wind.

Laurence walked blindly around and around the building, not seeing the shattered hulk but the days, the nights, the hopes, the patient dreams that had gone into it, and for the first time his heart went out of him.

You plead and beg and coax and ask people for help when they have so little and they give it to you, they give the very strength of their bodies and faith of their souls, and then—nothing but a shambles. He would not have the courage to ask them to start all over again.

At that moment any youthful cocksureness, childish pride, or arrogance that were left in the twenty-four-year-old man drained right out of his shoe soles into the brush-laden earth. He had never known such discouragement before.

Yancy finally called him in to breakfast, and mechanically Laurence sat down, munched on a piece of corn bread, downed a glass of milk, and stared unseeingly at the walls of the little cabin. Yancy's warm eyes were full of sympathy and several times he started to say something, but did not.

The day passed quietly. Neither the army of builders nor the students showed up. Nor was there a happy squad of women at noon with their baskets and their good cheer. Laurence and Yancy cleared away some of the worst wreckage around the cabin, more to keep busy than anything, and that night, after reading their Bibles, went to bed in silence.

All night long Laurence wrestled in his sleep, dreaming of Iowa, then of students on that log where he had begun his school. He woke up once sitting up in bed wondering how fifty of them could sit on that log.

The second morning after the storm, with a bright sun out, the young men were finishing their early-morning meal when they heard shouts and talking down the road.

"Reckon some of our students are coming back," Yancy said.

"Well," Laurence said with a sigh, "we'll just keep teaching them in here until the old cabin bursts its sides."

"Mornin', 'Fesser, we sho' had us a storm, diden' we?"

Laurence glanced up at the door and, to his surprise, saw Hector McLaurin standing there.

"Sorry I couldn't get by yestiddy," Hector continued, "but I had some fences down, and I had to get 'em fix' fust."

"You came back to work on the building?" Laurence asked dully.

"Sho' did," Hector said, turning to eye the smashed pine structure. "We's lucky it's still on its feet. Looks a mite crippled, but we kin be thankful it ain't plum down."

"There's Amon Gibson with his mules and wagon," Yancy cried excitedly.

Laurence rushed outside. Amon was driving carefully into the clearing, picking a path for the wagon among the fallen trees.

"Mornin', 'Fesser," he called cheerfully. "Ain't we lucky we's all been saved?"

"Your family is all right?" Laurence asked guiltily, suddenly realizing that in the overwhelming blow of the shattered building he had almost forgotten his friends.

"Yassuh," said Amon, "they's fine. In fact, I think the folks 'round hyear must be mighty good prayerers. We didn't lose a single one in these parts—man, woman, or chile. All dat screechin' and carryin' on, and all we lost was a few fences and some ole sheds and barns."

"No more'n what we could fix up in a day," said another farmer who joined them as he came from another direction into the clearing. He cast an eye at the lopsided pine structure. "Now how you figger we goin' to get that thing back up whar it b'longs?"

Laurence followed the man's gaze and, for the first time since the storm, he saw the battered building not as a lost hope but as a problem to tackle. "We'll have to have some jacks," he said briskly. "I imagine they have some we could borrow over at the sawmill or at the railroad station."

"Why don't you take this ole mule, 'Fesser, an' see what you kin get?" offered one man, who had come up leading a mule. "Rest of us fellers, we can start tidyin' up roun' hyear."

"Better take my team, 'Fesser," said Amon, "so if they loans you jacks you kin haul 'em right back up hyear."

"I'll take you and your team," Laurence said. "If those mules heard damnyankee orders, they'd sit right down in their harness."

"Jes' lissen." Amon laughed heartily, clapped the little 'Fesser's back, and the two men climbed in the wagon and drove off, the echo of good-natured laughter coming to them long after they were out of sight of the clearing. "You'll have all yo' workers back in a day or so," Amon said.

Laurence leaned back on the wagon seat, gazed at the benevolent blue sky above him, and sighed with a sense of new-found peace. Strange that but a few moments ago he had known the greatest dejection of his life, and now he was buoyed and lifted and humbled before all this evidence of good will. These people had so little to give, so they knew how to give the greatest of all gifts—the gift of the heart.

"I came to teach them," he thought, as the wagon bumped over the storm-strewn road, "I came to teach them and nothing I have ever known, or could tell them, could equal the lesson they have given me."

When Laurence and Amon returned a few hours later, with the jacks they had borrowed from the sawmill in the back of the wagon, Laurence could hardly believe what he saw. Though not yet noon, the "woman army" had already appeared, their baskets of food set in the cabin door, and the women themselves, in their voluminous skirts and aprons, were busily gathering stray roots, branches, and carrying them out of the clearing. The men had already cleared away the tangle from around the building and were doing what they could to get the lopsided building back into some semblance of its former shape.

Day after day followed each other again, weary days, and nights in which Laurence and Yancy worked by moonlight or the light of bonfires. Weeks went by, and then the building was finished.

"Why, I do believe it looks better than it did befo'," was the pleased conclusion that went from lip to lip.

The rough but serviceable two-story building was christened Taylor Hall, at John Webster's suggestion, in honor of Uncle Ed, and most of the activities of the school were moved into it. Now the old cabin was freed for sleeping quarters and office space.

With housing for eighty-five resident students, including some girls, and space for classes in reading, writing, sewing, cooking, and carpentering, Piney Woods Country Life School was now open for business.

Chapter 8

"He Sho' Pulled de Rag Off de Bush"

By New Year's Day, 1910, the school was in full operation. But as the winter days passed and spring came to the land, the visitors, both white and colored, who came to see what was happening would have thought it more of a frontier settlement rather than a school. By now there were eighty-five students, and when not attending class the boys were out clearing brush, chopping wood, preparing land for planting, or building temporary pens and sheds for poultry and stock. The meals were prepared by the girls, some of them working while others attended class.

Work-your-way education made sense to some of the students but not to others. One girl who came to the school from deep in the backwoods was disappointed to find that Piney Woods School "had no mo' clearin' than we got back home. It was smack in the woods." Another, whose duty it was to fetch water from the spring, complained in a letter home to an older brother that she "felt too poorly" for such hard work, and that she did not see what hauling water had to do with getting an education. Her brother wisely replied, "If you don't feel up to hauling a bucketful, leave the bucket at the top of the hill and carry the water to it by the cupful till you have it full."

To pay their tuition, students arrived with a jug of cane syrup, a sack of ground meal, a pig, or a calf. Georgia Lee Myers, the first girl boarding student enrolled, brought with her a variety of items which, since she had no parents or money and only a burning desire for education, she collected from friends and neighbors. Her list of contributions and the names of the donors included:

Aunt Hester Robinson—one pound of butter and a dime.
Grandma Willis—a chicken.

68

Aunt Lucy McCornell—four bits.
Sarah Pernell—a chicken.
Effie McCoy—a cake and five cents.
Sam McCoy—five cents.
James Buckner—two bits.
Mrs. Church—seven cents.
Meal Kye—two bits.
Mollice Pernell—"a few things."
Chlora Pernell—a dime.
Bessie Harvey—one of her dresses.
Washington Lincoln Johnson—two pecks of meal.
Mandy Willis—a dozen eggs.

Not a student that came had enough money to pay tuition and none of them could afford to pay board. In exchange for a few hours of class instruction each day they worked the land, fed and clothed themselves, and learned new methods as they labored.

Uncle Tom Brown, who appeared sporadically from his woods hideout for classes, was heard to comment as he walked back and forth over the busy clearing, with its two-story building, waving flag, and busy workers, "M-m-m-mus' be s-s-s-some k-k-k-kin' of gov'ment p-p-p-p-proposition!"

All of this bustling activity meant more work and worry for Laurence. True, he had won the confidence and respect of the colored people, but there still remained the knotty problem, literally walking a tightrope, of not stirring up the resentment of the whites which might mean the violent end of his project, and the knottier problem of raising enough money to keep the school going.

While his classes "read out" their lessons, or while some of the brighter ones helped out, Laurence sat at a table and wrote letter after letter North asking for funds. When he had finished the second batch of fifty he took them to the sawmill to address them.

"More appeals?" Webster asked.

"Yes."

"Well, come up here any time you want to use the machines," Webster said, "and"—he looked back, his hand on the door, as if with an afterthought—"you can use my stationery and envelopes if you wish. I'll have Manuel fix you up with stamps at the post office."

"Why, thank you, Mr. Webster," Laurence said.

"No need to." Webster turned his head away, seemingly embarrassed. "I figure any northern money you bring in here will help me, too." He quickly shut the door and walked rapidly away.

Laurence sat for a moment, his warm eyes following the figure of the man as it disappeared. Here at least, he thought, he had made a friend.

Out of this second batch of fifty letters Laurence received one reply. "Although I am supporting all the schools I can, your story appealed to me in a special way," it said. "Enclosed is a check for $15." Signed "Emily Howland." This sum did not go far toward feeding nearly a hundred people, Laurence knew, and yet it gave him hope. He felt that his, indeed, was a "special" story, a story that would gain support if presented properly.

More and more letters went out, laboriously written during school classes and addressed at the sawmill, nearly a thousand of them, and only one response. It had in it a check for $10 but what was far, far more important, this message: "I like what you are doing in your corner of the vineyard. May the Lord give you the desire of your heart."

It was signed, "Captain Asa Turner," and came from Iowa's great old farmer who had graduated from college at sixty-five and who after that had gone on to revolutionize the corn culture of the state and to scatter information and good will to thousands of people all over the country.

A few days later, as Laurence looked over his mail at the sawmill post office and stared with a longing eye at a great bowl of succulent pigs' knuckles in the little store, John Webster entered and came up to him.

"What kind of response did you get on that last batch of letters?" he asked.

Laurence had no intention of embroidering the truth. "One reply," he said.

"I'm afraid you're pulling uphill, Jones." Webster shook his head. "You're in the wrong part of the country—should have picked a large town or city, where you could get some local support from colored folks."

"That is where you are wrong, Mr. Webster," Laurence stated.

Webster's head came up sharply at this eye-to-eye speech, but his shock was lost in the rush of words that came from the young teacher's mouth.

"This is a country-life school, Mr. Webster. How could I demonstrate agriculture in a city? How could I even get a start in the city? I came here broke. Who would have helped me like you and Uncle Ed Taylor? I am in the right place. It's a good white community and a good colored community and it's up to me to win my place in it and put over the school. If I can't do it, I'll move on, but I won't have any city for my school."

The shock on Webster's face was replaced by a friendly smile. "I have no answer for that," he said simply. "I'd sure give you the blue medal for oratory."

The two men laughed together, and Laurence hurried away to the ten thousand jobs that awaited him at the school.

When he was out of sight, Webster's storekeeper, Manuel, wiped imaginary sweat off his forehead and said, "Whew! can't that nigger talk though!"

"Got me beat forty ways to Sunday," Webster admitted. "I'll say one thing, he don't lack for nerve, trying to run that school with all that passel of kids and no money or no sight of any."

"I've never seen him with a dime," Manuel confided. "He comes in here most every day after his mail, but he don't buy nothin'. No"—Manuel shook his head decisively—"he don't spend a cent and my personal opinion is he ain't *got* a cent!"

"You're probably right."

Manuel leaned farther over the counter and his voice became confidential. "Once he asked about the price of those pigs' feet," he said, "an' I done told him ten cents for a whole or five cents for a half."

"Did he buy one?" asked Webster.

"No, not him." Manuel shrugged. "He just thanked me and went on, but I see him lookin' at 'em mos' every time he comes in. Folks say they ain't eatin' nothin' but cowpeas and corn bread down at the school."

"Well," John Webster said quickly, "if he ever asks about those pigs' feet again, you tell him they're on the house—hear?"

Manuel's eyes shot up in surprise. "Yeah, Boss, I hear."

March, and the first signs of spring in the Piney Woods—green spikes of grass pushing up through the red earth, the first curled leaves of woods violets, the pale promise of dogwood in the deep forests. Spring and planting time. Laurence wished fervently that some of the odd and sundry "gifs" to the school had included a "live, working animal." Yes, spring meant planting, and the chance for food for the next winter might be dependent upon planting a garden now. But making a garden without a work animal was at the best a rough prospect. And all of the farmers, including Amon, were using the animals they had now.

Laurence and Yancy and William Dixon worked out plans for the garden—what they would plant, how they would care for it to the best advantage. They picked a rolling hill site below the cabin which the students had cleared of brush during the winter. Then Laurence and the older students laboriously plowed it by hand with the smaller ones following behind pulverizing the clods with hoes to prepare for the seed.

As they worked, Laurence talked, explaining to them what his plans were—plans that they in turn could carry home to instruct their fathers and neighbors by, and which they could follow themselves.

"How come we's plantin' 'roun' de hill?" one boy wanted to know.

"This is contour plowing," Laurence explained. "You see we go with the earth, making ridges that will catch and hold the water when the rains come, and not only nourish the crops but will also keep the water from washing the soil down the hill and ruining the land which we must depend on for our food."

Corn—from the very best of the seed which had been selected and saved from the year before. Cowpeas, of course, an old staple that made up for the lack of meat. Cane for syrup; all the hardy greens—turnip and kale and collards and mustard; tomatoes, beets, sweet potatoes—food to can and to store in bins. Laurence hoped that by fall he would have some first-class home-economics instruction for the girls. So far all he had been able to give them was general rules for sanitation and household instruction which came from farm magazines and guides. Next year, if the garden worked out, they would have more variety of food both to eat and to cook with—something beyond the endless peas and corn bread which had made up their winter's diet and which every cabin girl knew how to cook with her eyes shut.

As he worked in the garden and cornfield, with Yancy and the boys, plowing and hoeing in the warm spring sun, Laurence paused occasionally to rest on his hoe or plow handles, to look up past the school building to the densely thicketed hilltop above—his land, part of that original forty acres; and in his mind, with ambitious visions for the future where the Piney Woods school would someday be. He could even squint his eyes against the sun glare now and envision it—the cedar brake cleared away, the hilltop covered with a sprinkling of dignified buildings, a circular road, an industrial shop for the boys, a model kitchen for the girls, all laid out in a sort of a neat horseshoe arrangement. . . .

"Dreamin' again?" Yancy teased.

"Planning." Laurence smiled.

"Still aimin' to take over the Dog-eaters' ha'nt?" Yancy asked in fun.

Although he had spoken to Laurence in a low voice, one of the younger boys working a row near them looked up, his eyes suddenly widened with fright.

"You ain't really fixin' to take us all up thar with the Dog-eater, is you, 'Fesser?" he asked, his voice edged with pleading.

Laurence studied the boy's white-eyed look. His fright was obviously real. "You believe the Dog-eater lives on that hill?" he asked.

"Co'se I do," the boy said. "Lots of folks has seen him!"

"What does he look like?" Laurence prompted.

The boy put down his hoe, the better to use his hands for his description. "He 'bout dis high"—he held his hands nearly eighteen inches from the ground—"and he about dis long." He spread his arms as far as they could reach, measuring over five feet along the ground.

So far the story was about the same as that the other children had told. The Dog-eater obviously looked like an outsized dachshund.

"Does he have a head like a dog?" Laurence asked.

The boy thought a minute, scratching thoughtfully behind one ear. "Mo' like a wolf," he decided, "or mebbe a dragon. He got big fangs." He made a low curve under his own jaw to show the length of the Dog-eater's lethal teeth. "An' he lives on puppy dogs, and if'n he cain't get 'em, he eats chillun," he finished triumphantly.

"Well," Laurence said, "I promise you I'll clear out the Dog-eater along with the brush before I take you up there."

May—and closing time. Without farm machinery the children were needed at home to chop cotton and help get the crops going.

Although there were no graduates from his first year's operation Laurence decided to have commencement exercises to keep interest alive in the school. To allay any suspicions and to satisfy the curiosity about "jes' what been goin' on down at that there nigger school," he sent out invitations to the whites for miles around, from the little town of Braxton to as far away as Jackson. Instinctively, he realized that his safety and his opportunity to continue lay in public knowledge of "jes' what was goin' on"—the best ammunition against the dangerous mouth-to-ear gossip.

Jones, with the help of Yancy and Dixon, worked many long hours figuring out a program that might interest the people. The night of the commencement he realized that if anything he had underestimated southern curiosity. The big main room of Taylor Hall, which doubled as a chapel and classroom, was packed to overflowing, with the white section surprisingly crowded, considering that they had no children to applaud. Laurence was pleased to see the large figure of his friend John Webster in the front row of the white section.

"Do you think they'll cotton to this, 'Fesser, or do you think it might make any of 'em mad?" whispered Yancy.

Laurence examined the face of his young helper and saw that he was extremely nervous, a rivulet of sweat pouring down each cheek in front of his ears, and he clasped and unclasped his hands.

"Certainly it is right," Laurence assured him gravely. "There is no other way."

"But you don't know these folks like I do," Yancy said, his teeth chattering. "You think you got 'em with you and then they may turn 'round and set the place afire. You know what they all say about educating niggers." Yancy looked straight at Laurence. "You aren't scared, 'Fesser? You aren't nervous?"

Laurence smiled, his face set in the odd lines of peace and far-seeing reassurance. "No, I'm not nervous," he said. "When anything is as needed as this is, it can't go wrong."

Yancy stared a second longer into Laurence's dreamy, withdrawn eyes, rich with their private faith. "Lawd a-mercy, 'Fesser," he said, laughing, "I think these woods folks are right when they claim the Lord's got a hand on you!"

"Come on," Laurence said, "let's begin."

Yancy stepped out from behind an improvised curtain, held up his hand for silence, then at a signal from him the cheap pine rafters rang with "Onward, Christian Soldiers."

After the song, Uncle Ed Taylor led them in the Lord's Prayer, then the curtain to the makeshift stage was pulled and commencement began!

As the curtain lifted, a mutter of surprise ran through the audience. On the stage was an ironing board, a sewing table, a laundry tub, a workbench, and a stove. Before the amazed eyes of the audience boys and girls in neat aprons and overalls took their places on the stage. One girl began mixing batter, another unrolled a bolt of cloth on the table and started to cut out a dress, a boy settled down at the workbench repairing harness, and another worked on a wagon wheel. Two youngsters sat cross-legged in a corner of the stage weaving straw mats.

One by one the students came forward, explained in brief terms what they were doing, what they had learned to do at school the past year, and what techniques, information, and work habits they were illustrating by their particular job. There were no orations, no meaningless rhetorical phrases, no fanfare. Each student explained his job, then illustrated it by doing it before the audience.

A sudden squeal in the aisle turned the heads of the startled audience toward a small, earnest black boy who was making his way to the stage with a protesting pig in his arms. The audience howled, but there was no laughter on the boy's serious face. When he got his unruly pig to the stage, he faced the audience and announced soberly, "This hyear's a good pig. An' I gonna tell y'all the diff'ence 'tween him an' a ole razorback like we mos'ly got—the diff'unce in health, in cost of raising, an' in the meat we gets from him." Grasping the squealing animal firmly around the neck, the boy proceeded with his lecture.

By the time the boy and the pig had relinquished the stage, the first batch of ginger cookies had come out of the oven and now their cook, smiling from under her immaculate white cap, walked down from the stage with a plate of the farm cookies and passed them out to the audience to sample, while she explained the ingredients she had used, and described the baking process.

As the straw mats were completed they, too, were presented to members of the audience to pass around, to feel, to test, while their manufacture was explained.

From an initial wide-eyed amazement the atmosphere of the audience, both in the white and the colored section, changed to one of jocular neighborly interest as they passed the products from hand to hand, with comments on the job. By the time the last ginger cake and biscuit had been sampled, the last exhibit presented, it was a laughing, joking, talking crowd of people that had been thoroughly entertained.

Finally, Laurence stepped to the stage, thanked his guests for their attention, congratulated his students for the year's work, and with a final hymn the first commencement of the Piney Woods Country Life School came to a triumphal close.

The man next to John Webster turned, slapped him on the arm, and said, "Why, durned if it wasn't jus' like that Jones said—he said he was goin' to learn 'em how to work, and blame me if he hasn't done it!"

"Never saw anything like it befo'," cried another, shaking his head in admiration. "Haven't had so much fun in a coon's age."

"Beats all I ever did see," agreed a third as he helped his neighbor up from his chair.

As the people in the white section filed out into the warm spring night, offering friendly congratulations as they went, Laurence smiled thoughtfully to himself. "Seems like a good nigger," he heard a man say. This was an accolade for the South and was one which Laurence had every intention of building on. Someday, perhaps, they would say, "He seems like a good man."

As the last of the colored people were leaving, Laurence heard an old woman say, "Lawsy, de 'Fesser, he sho' pulled de rag off de bush."

Chapter 9

"The Wit to Win"

Love and I had the wit to win
We drew a circle that took him in.
—Markham

Word of the commencement at Piney Woods quickly reached the ears of all the local folk who had not been able to attend. Everywhere Laurence went—to Braxton, to Jackson, or even on the local roads at some distance away—he was greeted with a warm, friendly respect and given encouraging nods and smiles. Right now his stock, he realized, was high. He had promised that his school would "suit the white folks," and he had made good on his promise. But he was not foolish enough to believe that this momentary approval meant that he could do what he pleased or that it would last indefinitely. It would be a position to be constantly rewon, a battle to be refought daily. In a country where a Negro was not supposed to read and write, and most especially not to "figger," "larnin' niggers" would, for a long time, be looked upon with suspicion. The psychology of the deep South was not yet ready to let the tradition of slavery—the inferiority of the slave and the superiority of the master—give way to common justice and ordinary human rights which democracy indicated.

At the moment, to whip up these historic hatreds, white-supremacy advocate James K. Vardaman, ex-governor, dressed in a white suit, was once again driving his white lumber wagon drawn by white oxen through the farm areas of Mississippi, poisoning the air with anti-Negro speeches, in his campaign for a seat in the United States Senate.

The young teacher's only answer to the Vardaman threat was to consolidate his own gains on the home front. The more familiar the

local whites were with the school, the more they understood its
teacher, the less apt they would be to turn against it at the incitation
of a rabble-rousing outsider. Laurence tried to make certain that
within the limits of his knowledge and instincts he did nothing to
offend the whites, particularly those whites of such a low economic
level that they lived in constant fear that their Negro neighbors
might get things that they could not. On the road between Piney
Woods and the village of Braxton there lived two poor white families,
good people but ground down by poverty and ignorance. During
either planting or harvesting seasons, when these farmers and their
families were out working in the fields, Laurence made it a point
not to walk by the road in front of their places. If he was forced to
go to Braxton on business, at those times he went down back of the
school and walked down the railroad tracks that led into the village
without being seen by these people. A "dressed-up" colored man,
walking along "doin' nothin'," while white folks had to work, would
have been an angering sight for those in the field.

But now, with the school year over, he had an even more pressing
problem than getting along with the white neighbors. And this was
money. Eleven hundred letters and only two replies! Singularly
hopeful, those two, but they did not solve the immediate problem
of the support of the school. However, they had given Laurence a
clue. His story, to the two who had answered, seemed unique. The
problem was to get its uniqueness and its importance through to the
attention and hearts of many more. Laurence felt his answer probably lay in direct person-to-person contact. This had worked with
John Webster. It should also work in the North.

He borrowed enough money from Uncle Ed to buy day-coach fare
to Iowa.

When he walked into the ticket office an hour ahead of traintime
there were several people in line and Laurence stood back, waiting
his turn. Eventually the other customers had been served and he
stepped up, holding his money in his hand, and said,

"One-way day-coach ticket to Keokuk, Iowa."

The station agent was writing something on a pad in front of him
and seemed not to hear. Laurence repeated his request. The man
turned and walked through a door into the back of the office. Laurence waited. Finally he heard laughter and joking, and when he

peered through the half-opened door into the back room he saw the ticket seller sitting on a table, talking to another employee.

Laurence looked at the station clock. He had now been in the waiting room for forty minutes and the train was nearly due.

"Would you please wait on me?" he called out, trying to keep his voice courteous.

The man turned, stared through the door at him. "Take it easy, boy," he answered, and turned back to his friend.

The bills crackled in Laurence's hands as his fists automatically clenched. Then he wet his lips, counted ten, and tried again. "I'd like to catch this train," he said quietly.

The ticket seller looked at him in surprise, then the sight of the roll of bills seemed to remind him of a possible sale. He ambled back to the window.

"What'ya want, Sam?"

In the distance Laurence could hear the whistle of the approaching train. "One way to Keokuk," he said through clenched teeth.

With maddening deliberation the ticket seller made out the ticket, pushed it under the window, took the money, and made change. By now the train was pulling into the station. His eye on the train, Laurence picked up his bag, held out his hand for his change. A whistling noise went past his ear, and he heard the coins strike as they hit the far corner of the waiting room. With impotent fury he stared from the waiting train outside to his scant supply of money which now lay in the dirt in the corner. Then he rushed to the corner, scooped up the coins, and ran outside, clambering up the steps just as the train pulled out of the station.

The front half of the Jim Crow car doubled as a smoker. Beyond that, roughly curtained off by a canvas drape and the heavy smoke-clouded air, huddled the occupants—sweaty laborers, young women with small babies, evil-eyed ruffians, a smattering of carefully dressed men and women, children of all ages—crowded together in this one end of the car. All carried some sack or container with cold food sufficient to last the length of their trip.

Laurence squeezed himself into a corner near the window, pocketed his change, and wiped the dirt from his hands. His encounter had left him trembling with anger, and as he looked about him he realized that this "ride" promised little respite. He had even forgot-

ten to fortify himself with sandwiches. He leaned back against the
dirty cushion and shielded his eyes with his hands. Once more he
realized what a difficult role he had chosen. To "take low" in the
interests of the job he wished to do—no matter what the insult.
Boyishly he thought of what a joy it would have been to cut loose
and tell that insolent rascal just what he thought. And yet, the young
teacher sighed wistfully, the goal he had set himself did not allow
the luxury of temper. Or protest. He thought of the ring of patient
farmers who had appeared the second day after the big storm . . .
the faces of his students, so eager for a chance they had never
hoped to have. . . . Whenever his anger or indignation began boiling
up, he would think of them. One false move, and he would betray
an awesome trust. . . .

Laurence reached Keokuk on a Saturday afternoon with no plans
on how or where to begin. As he walked from the station to a
boardinghouse to which a porter had directed him he passed by a
broom factory.

He paused and looked through a window into the busy shop where
he could see machines and men working at them. Making brooms
was one of the projects he had in the back of his mind for Piney
Woods. It was a simple enough trade to learn, once you had a
machine, and there certainly ought to be a market for the finished
product in the Piney Woods country where most brooms were
homemade from dogwood branches, wild sedge, and tied with
creepers. Hurrying on up the street, he found his boardinghouse,
checked in, and left his bag, then came back to the broom factory.

The owner, after Laurence had told him about his school, showed
him around the plant, pointing out the various operations that went
into the making of brooms, and explained to him how the machines
worked. There was one machine standing idle in the corner of the
room.

"Would you sell it to me?" Laurence asked.

"I guess so," the owner said. "We haven't been using it lately."

"How much?"

"Oh, I'd say $35."

"Will you hold it for me for a week?"

"S'pose so." The man shrugged. "I'm not anxious to get rid of it
anyhow."

Laurence stayed on until the shop closed, picking up all the pointers he could about the manufacture of brooms—enough, he hoped, to be able to demonstrate to the students back home and start some of them at this trade.

The next morning was Sunday, and Laurence dressed himself as neatly as he could and made the rounds of the churches asking permission to tell his story. After three of them turned him down, the pastor of the fourth invited him in on the condition that he would not take up a collection.

As he told his story to a large Bible class, emphasizing the need for the school in improving the condition of the Negroes, he watched the rows of faces before him to see if they betrayed any reaction to the story he was trying to get across to them, the story he was attempting to tell in Christian terms of human salvage and human life.

When he had finished, there was a polite patter of applause and then the members of the class filed out to go into the main sanctuary for the service. As Laurence watched them leave, discouragement gripped him. He had a story to tell, of that he was certain—a story that differed from the ordinary appeal, but somehow he had not gotten it over to this group in such a way that it either won their enthusiastic attention or their support. Then he saw one man, the last to leave, turn back to look at him, and, as if on impulse, he darted back.

"Here," he said almost furtively, thrusting a dollar bill into the young teacher's hand. "I was interested in what you had to say." He turned to leave.

"Wait," Laurence begged. "Do you think there are other men in Keokuk who would be interested also?"

The man paused, thought a minute, then took a Sunday-school program out of his pocket, a pencil from his vest, and started to scribble across the back of it.

"I'll give you the names of some of the leading businessmen around here," he said, "but don't tell 'em I sent you!"

The next morning, his first prospect, the owner of a hardware store, listened politely, then said, "I like what you say, young man, and I'll tell you what I'll do. You go talk to Mr. Huiskamp—he's pretty hard to fool—and if he goes along with you, I will also."

At first Laurence was puzzled. And then it occurred to him that in most cities, as Mr. Webster back at Piney Woods, there were certain kingpins, certain leaders, that the others followed. Getting Mr. Huiskamp to back him might just be the "open sesame" to the rest of the businessmen in the city. He made a few cautious inquiries among the colored men and found out that his conjecture was right. Huiskamp was the owner and manager of a large manufacturing business and the leading businessman of the community.

Out at Mr. Huiskamp's factory Laurence discovered that his prospect was out. He received a grudging permission to wait until the man he wanted to see returned, which was not for several hours. After another wait Laurence was granted an interview.

He walked into the office, with a silent prayer, stood before Mr. Huiskamp's desk and, as soon as his presence was acknowledged, launched into his plea for help. The factory owner listened patiently and with some degree of interest, but when Laurence finished, he spread his hands on the desk with a gesture of pseudo-apology— "I'm sorry, but to state it bluntly, I'm 'given out' for the year. It seems like everybody has come along at the same time." He nodded briskly. "Thank you, anyway, and I wish you luck."

The interview was obviously over. Laurence stood a second, staring dazedly at the man, then mumbled his thanks for the courtesy of the interview and stumbled out to the street before the first sickening wave of despair wiped the polite smile off his face.

As he stood uncertainly in the street he looked back at the factory, then at the sky. It was already nearly dusk. Too late to try to see anyone else. He fingered the change in his pocket, felt his thin wallet, and thought that he would be lucky if he stirred up enough to get to the next town.

When Laurence got back to his room, he decided to go to bed at once. Since the day was over as far as business contacts were concerned, he might try to go to sleep. In that way he would not miss supper so much. He undressed and lay in the dusk thinking, and, as was his wont, praying quietly, sincerely, and without embarrassment. He needed help and needed it badly, for somehow he had failed.

Then, as he thought back once more over the day's events, rehashing what he had said, studying to find the clue to his failure,

Laurence suddenly sat up in bed, stirred by a disturbing picture that took shape in his mind. He had had a challenge and he had muffed it. That man was his key. To miss him meant to miss the entire town. There had to be a way to get through. Without knowing quite what he intended to do, Laurence got out of bed, put on his clothes, and went down to the street. He stopped at a telephone booth and looked up Huiskamp's home address, then started walking.

By the time he reached Huiskamp's house, many blocks from his boardinghouse, his emotional momentum was even greater than when he started. Without pausing he marched up the steps of the big house and pressed the doorbell. A moment's wait, and then the door came open, and there was Mr. Huiskamp, coat off, house slippers on, and the evening paper in his hand.

"Mr. Huiskamp," Laurence said, his voice husky with urgency, "I've got to talk to you."

The factory owner stared at Laurence, his eyes narrowed in annoyance. "Aren't you the same young fellow who came to my office this afternoon?"

"Yes, I am," Laurence said, feeling the hot blood rise in his cheeks, "but I feel there were things I didn't tell you. Please give me a chance to talk to you, Mr. Huiskamp."

The man was obviously irritated, but there was something in the desperate sincerity in the young teacher's taut, flushed face framed by the door light, something so urgent in the depths of his eyes, his voice, that it got through to the man, past the barricade of his annoyance. "I don't want to talk to you here now," he said gruffly, "but you can come around to my office again tomorrow. I'll see you then." He shut the door.

As he turned away from the closed door and half-stumbled down the steps toward the black street below, a wave of nausea swept over Laurence, causing him to reach for an iron fence to lean on for support. He clung to it for a moment, fighting down the sudden weakness, then walked slowly back toward his boardinghouse.

He had done it! Something as foreign to his own nature as anything he had ever done in his life. He had begged a man for a chance. Not only begged, but pestered and pursued, trailing him into the privacy of his own home. All of Laurence's instincts shrank from anything so brazen and debased.

Yet he had had no choice. This man was his key to the other men in the city. And, Laurence decided, as he walked slowly back toward his room, if a cause is legitimate, perhaps even begging was permissible—if done with dignity. He was not asking for himself; he was asking for humanity.

True to his word, Mr. Huiskamp gave him another hearing the next day as well as a small check. This victory meant a highroad to the other men on his list as well as to others suggested to him. By the end of the week he had raised enough money to purchase and ship the broom-making machine back to Piney Woods, to send a small sum to Uncle Ed against his debt, and to have enough left over to get to Des Moines.

A friend of his at the university, now a lawyer, had arranged for him to speak before a civic club in that city. But when they got to the meeting only a few men had turned out to hear his talk. Laurence made his plea as forcefully as he knew how, but it produced only a pitifully small amount in contributions.

"I was watching closely, Laurence," his friend said when they were alone, "and when you got to the part where you described some of your actual experiences down in the piney woods your listeners began to sit up and take notice."

"Perhaps I should build my talk around them," Laurence broke in. "I hadn't thought that they would be of interest to people."

"You are wrong," his friend advised. "It's the personal touch that interests them. A racial problem or an educational problem or any generalized talk on poverty in the deep South, or anywhere else, is something that they hear all the time. But they will laugh or cry if you'll tell about the things that happened to you down there, because that makes the problem personal to them."

"You're right," Laurence said, brightening as he thought about some of the things he had gone through. "And the Lord knows enough things have happened to make it interesting. I can work up an entire speech around my experiences and only bring in the needs incidentally."

"That is the idea," his friend said.

By the time Laurence appeared before his next audience he was "loaded for bear." As he swayed them back and forth, alternately between a good laugh and tears, he not only softened their hearts but their pocketbooks. The meeting netted him a tidy sum and an excellent list of names to call upon with the way prepared.

A businessman, the father of another of his classmates, gave him more valuable advice.

"You have an appealing story," he said, "and I am going to help you. But if you expect to get regular financial support out of businessmen be sure to keep your facts and your records straight. Never lie, and never embellish your story, because if any businessman once catches you in a lie, he will sour on you and never support you again."

"What sort of records do you mean, sir?" he asked.

"Keep an accurate record of all income, all outgo, and have a regular annual audit," he said. "Then you will have a financial statement which you will be able to show at any time. It will reassure the businessman, in terms he understands, about where his money is going, and whether or not the funds are being handled wisely. If he is convinced your school is 'good business' he will be much more apt to support it generously."

This made good sense to Laurence. He realized that he needed not single donations but regular contributors who could be counted on from year to year. If they assumed the responsibility for the school's maintenance, they certainly had a right to know exactly how its finances were handled.

As he moved from town to town, Laurence's confidence increased and his skill as a solicitor took shape. He spoke before church groups, luncheon clubs, civic organizations, and several times even at private parties.

One afternoon he was standing in front of a bank building in Cedar Rapids, Iowa, when he saw a lion-maned old man drive by in an electric car.

"Who is that?" he asked a man standing near him.

"That is Mr. Douglas—president of the Starch Works."

Next morning, shortly after nine, Laurence was at the Starch Works office with a request that he be allowed to see Mr. George Douglas.

To his surprise he was granted an immediate interview. He walked in, paused a timid moment as he faced the huge, aristocratic old gentleman, and then, girding up his courage, told his story of the neglected Negro children in the woods, with the emphasis on what he had done about it.

Douglas asked several pointed questions about how he intended to run the school and to handle his funds; what he was going to do for a faculty; what sort of buildings he expected to put up. When Laurence had answered to his apparent satisfaction the old man pulled open his desk drawer, took out his checkbook, and filled in a check.

"I like your ideas, Mr. Jones," he said with a keen glance at the young man before him. "They sound practical. I wish you luck. Come back to see me again."

He tore out the check and handed it to Laurence. Laurence took it, thanked Mr. Douglas, and left. The check was for $50.

Two days later, when Laurence was standing in a bank getting a draft for the money he had collected so he could send it to the bank at Braxton, he felt a heavy hand on his shoulder, and, turning, saw Mr. Douglas standing beside him.

"You know, Mr. Jones," he said thoughtfully, "the job you are trying to do has stayed in my mind, and I have regretted that I didn't give you more when you were in my office. I'd like to add this, and God bless you."

He pressed a bill into Laurence's hand and strode off before the startled young man could thank him. Laurence stared at the crisp piece of paper in his hand and gasped. It was the first one-hundred-dollar bill he had ever seen.

Laurence wound up his Iowa venture with a broom-making machine, clear of his debt to Uncle Ed, several hundred dollars toward the next year's operating expenses, and enough to get himself and a new faculty member back to Piney Woods.

In Des Moines he had run into a former acquaintance, an artistic and intellectual young colored man named Louis Watson, who had found no niche for his talents beyond being a hotel porter. Unlike most northern Negroes who feared the South, Louis was fascinated with the life that Laurence described at Piney Woods and was eager to do something more important for the world than carry baggage. He decided to go back with Laurence, with no hope of salary nor even good food, but with an enthusiasm for helping a mass of eager children.

Chapter 10

"There Is a Balm in Gilead"

In September 1910, the second year of the Piney Woods School opened with five teachers—all under thirty—and more than a hundred students. Besides its principal, Laurence, there was Louis Watson and Yancy who, in addition, had married a young teacher and brought her back to help, and another young woman, a former student of Laurence when he had taught in Hinds County named Doschia Weathersby.

The addition of the two women teachers made it possible to add a "training kitchen" which offered to the girls advanced training in cooking as well as better food for everyone. A second check from Emily Howland, the woman who had been Piney Woods' first donor, came in with the request that a hand press be bought and a school paper be put out so that she could receive regular news about what was happening at the school.

The press was duly installed in the little cabin where Laurence still lived, and he personally used it to instruct students in the art of printing as well as for putting out school reports. One of the first things printed was a letter from an aunt of Georgia Lee Myers, describing her reaction to her niece's progress at Piney Woods:

"I am glad to write and tell you about the improvement you has made in Georgia, she is better in the washtub and in the fields and in the kitchen and in the house. She is better everywhere I puts her than she was. She has work so faithful sence she come home that I wants to send her back."

Some of the older men, satisfied with a smattering of "readin' an' writin'," had dropped out. But William Dixon was still there, as were Laurence's original trio of "log boys" who were now sophisticated second-year students. Uncle Tom still haunted the clearing, toting his musket, between classes, as self-appointed watchman of the school grounds.

87

"Is that gun loaded?" Laurence asked his "guard" one day in a teasing tone.

"J-j-j-jes' l-l-let s-s-s-some old varmint t-t-try to sneak up and t-t-t-tech s-s-s-somefin' b-b-b-belongs to dis s-s-s-school, an' we'll s-s-s-see ef it's l-l-l-loaded!" declared the old man, with a fierce grip on his treasured weapon.

Laurence's inner laughter vanished in the face of such touching loyalty. He thanked his old guard gently and went on his way.

On opening day, as he stood before the rows of eager young faces, many of them betraying the curiosity and half-fear of the new students for whom this was a strange and awesome experience, Laurence thought back to his own first day at school, and his heart warmed with sympathy for the timid brown children. His mother had taken him to the old Lincoln School in St. Joseph, introduced him to "Miss Sadie," and left. Small for his age, terrified at the crush of bigger, older children, Laurence had huddled down in his seat, tears stinging his eyes, so over all miserable that Miss Sadie had asked him what was wrong. "I'm tired and hungry and sleepy and my Mama needs me," he had blurted out in one hot, agonized breath. And the wise teacher had summoned an older boy to "carry him home," saying, "Any boy with that many things wrong with him ought to go home and come to school another day." He had arrived at home on the back of the other boy barely ten minutes after his mother had gotten there. The next day he had stuck it out, but he never looked out over the frightened, curious faces of "first students" without a warm and amused compassion.

He greeted the students, then spoke to them in simple words of what they might expect at Piney Woods.

"You will find that our course of study is planned with thoughts of teaching what will be the best for you. There are courses in agriculture, morals, and manners, the Bible, rural economics, arithmetic as it is used in everyday life, the chemistry of the farm and the home—these are what you will be trained in here.

"You have come here to seek freedom not from the kind of slavery your parents endured, but from a slavery of ignorance of mind and awkwardness of body. You have come for your soul's freedom. You have come to educate your head, your hands, and your heart. You want to know how to think clearly, how to live in the right way, and how to make some material progress in the world."

The children before him, warmed by the kindness of his smile, stirred by the promise of his words, began to relax and look forward to the days ahead.

As he acquired teachers to take over specific classes and trades, Laurence more and more confined his own work to the "morals and manners"—the spiritual growth of his students. He led the Bible classes, gave the Sunday chapel talks, was available at all hours, for advice or counsel. Young as he was, the children were drawn to him by far more than educational ties. He was their teacher, their guide, their friend; he was the common "father" who had come to bring them a chance for a life they had not known existed. His very presence seemed to provoke in the neglected children a desire to be "good," "honest," "thrifty," and "kind." As one student later described the feeling they all had for their 'fessor: "You could not look into eyes like that and lie."

For his share of work Louis Watson took over a section of classes in basic reading and writing and the role of bookkeeper for the school. Though money was too meager for much figuring, he kept a complete record of the grades and work time of all the students as they piled up hours which would pay for future classes.

Young Watson, as Laurence before him, was both fascinated and horrified, as the holiday season approached, with the Christmas plans of the woods folks for their traditional frolics. The extreme poverty which the past few years, with the aid of the boll weevil, had brought meant scarcely "fireworks" money this year, let alone "gifs" or delicacies.

"Let's give them a real Christmas," Louis suggested impulsively one night as he and Laurence sat up late at their desks in the cabin, Watson over his books, Laurence tinkering with the little press which he intended to use to save many hours of work in writing letters to the friends of the school.

"Maybe we can bring in a tree from the woods and decorate it," Laurence said, "and of course we will have chapel services. But we haven't any money for gifts. Any money we have must go for food."

"I'll figure something," Louis said, his eyes dreamy. "I'd like to show these poor little kids what Christmas can mean."

"Do what you wish," Laurence said, "just so it doesn't cost anything."

A few weeks later Laurence regretted that he had granted Watson the permission. The young man, his thin, sensitive face alight with a vision, was working on his project with feverish intensity. Each night, after a strenuous day of teaching and office work, he stayed up till nearly morning, working on his "Christmas boxes." He had written home to his mother in Iowa for tiny candles and what tree decorations she could stir up. The rest he was making by hand. A talented artist, he worked out hand-designed motto cards for each child which he laboriously lettered by hand, then decorated with painted borders of trailing holly and mistletoe. The "boxes," made of pasteboard and colored tissue, were also individually made with children's names in gleaming reds and greens and silver, the sides decorated with hand-painted Christmas scenes.

As Watson labored nightly over his designs the other teachers caught the spirit and began working on an *a capella* concert, selecting Christmas songs, and rehearsing them with the students.

As Christmas day approached and news spread through the community about the school party, Laurence wondered how it would appeal in comparison to the frolics of former years.

Drawn by either curiosity or "nothing at home," people of all ages began pouring into the school grounds on Christmas morning, although the program was not scheduled until afternoon. They all came—from graybearded oldsters to the smallest, newest babies no more than blanketed mounds in their mothers' arms. By noon the chapel of Taylor Hall was bursting with Christmas visitors and guests.

That day, for the first time, the Piney Woods folks traded their fireworks and whisky and smoke-filled rooms for a simple sermon and a concert of sacred music. As Laurence spoke to them, looking out over the hushed crowd, he saw eyes that feasted with heart-warming pleasure on the stage that was decked with pine and cedar boughs. If he had any doubts at all they were dispelled when he listened as they joined wholeheartedly in the religious music, lifting their voices in "Glory Hallelujah to De Newborn King," then crooning with a softer joy, "Mary Had a Baby." He knew that a genuine Christmas spirit had found a place in their lives and was thankful that Louis Watson had suggested the services.

And then the Christmas tree!

How all the little brown folks gasped and shrieked with pleasure when the curtains were parted and they saw their first Christmas tree—a tall, stately pine shimmering with the myriad lights of a hundred candles, bright with colored balls, and trailing "snow." At its base all of Watson's gaily-decorated Christmas boxes lay, filled with candy and nuts, each one bearing the name of a child.

For Laurence this was the happiest and the most miserable Christmas he had ever spent.

That Louis Watson had literally worked himself to death to create this joyful scene was a tragic aftermath of the holiday. Two weeks after Christmas—his frail constitution weakened by poor diet, the drafty cabin, and his own exhausting enthusiasm for bringing joy to these poor children—Louis died.

As Laurence wired Watson's mother, then shipped the body home, he realized that in his poverty and his dedication to the school he could not accompany his friend's body for its last rites. He knew also that Louis would have understood.

This was the first human life that went into the creation of Piney Woods.

To the four shocked fellow workers that Louis left behind his death meant a renewal of a dedication that must never be found lagging.

Chapter 11

"'Fesser Got a Hand"

Despite the sadness of losing his young associate, the pressure of money worries, the problems of feeding his "flock," Laurence made certain that winter that he did not neglect his white neighbors. Good neighbors, for him, truly meant "good fences"—against the ever-present threat of the southern social climate.

When he had first discovered clever young Yancy's varying talents: at carpentry, veterinary work, and farming, Laurence had put his young colleague at the "use of the community"—to be called on by any farmer, white or colored, any time he was needed for help or advice about a building, his stock, trees, or vegetable garden. Whenever Principal Jones heard of an illness or a death in a neighboring house, he dispatched a couple of students to chop firewood, cook, or nurse, till the crisis was past. When there was any sort of program scheduled at the school, he sent out generous invitations that included the entire countryside, white and colored. And any day, at any hour, visitors were welcome to "come see what they're doing in the woods."

If there was any work to be done at Piney Woods for which the school could afford to pay but which the students were unable to do, Laurence hired some local man so that he could come and not only do the job, but become acquainted with the school, and carry what he saw back home.

One hard-bitten old fellow whom Laurence hired, by chance, for a minor job, the teacher later discovered had one time suggested "let's string up that uppity nigger" but, after spending an afternoon at Piney Woods, reversed his opinion and decided, "I do b'lieve that feller's doin' some good out there."

Laurence's Iowa trip paid off in another way. Everyone he talked to he asked to send things they had no use for to the school. All

during the winter the boxes came in. They contained books, magazines, used clothes, and blankets. Laurence and his teachers carefully sorted out these things, writing itemized thanks to each donor,
then they distributed to the students what they could use. There
were a great many things that came in, however, that were not
usable by the children or the school. A quantity of men's topcoats
and suits, some women's evening dresses, hats, and jewelry. Figuring these things did the school no good lying in boxes, Laurence
decided to put them up for local sale, or, more correctly, barter.
The school could always use food. So he sorted out the goods, then
sent word around to the local colored farmers and their wives that
the following Saturday they could come with farm produce—eggs,
syrup, meal, chickens—and trade for the merchandise.

Quite a showing turned up, and he disposed of his first batch of
merchandise for several dollars in cash and enough food to feed his
school for a week.

With boxes arriving regularly, he decided to launch this as a
regular custom, and assigned one of the women teachers to handle
the goods as they came in, distribute what could be used to the
students, and dispose of the rest to the people in the community.

Later in the year, after several successful "sales" had been conducted, word reached Laurence that a needy white farmer had been
curious about where his colored neighbor got his warm winter coat.
Sensing that this was a handmade opportunity to further good will,
Laurence quickly sent out word to the white community that everyone was welcome to come and buy—or barter—for whatever struck
their fancy.

It was not long before the poor folks of Piney Woods of both
colors were spending a comfortable winter wrapped up in the cast-
off warm coats and suits of northern businessmen.

One day John Webster, on his way home from his office, ran into
a sight that made him catch his breath in amazement. It was a poor
white farmer he had known for many years bundled up in a beautiful
banker's special with a high fur collar which curled up around his
ears.

"Where did you get that overcoat?" asked Webster.

"Down't the nigger school," the old man said gleefully. "Paid a
dollar fo' it!"

Webster shook his head in amazement and walked on. It was a fabulous coat easily worth $25 secondhand. He wondered where "that Crazy Jones" had gotten the coat. But then he remembered how Jones had gotten ten thousand feet of lumber once, and he decided there was no need to ask.

Again, as winter softened into spring, more work was put in on the garden with the boys spending about half their time there. More land had been cleared, and it would be needed. There would be more students next year and more food would be eaten. Above all, Laurence felt the need for a work animal to help. But a mule cost $150 and he just did not have the money. He and Yancy put their heads together and decided that they could spare $20 toward buying an animal if they could find one for that. They scoured the country and finally found a little jinny that had been trained for harness. She was slow going, but a far sight better than pushing the plow by hand. Literally, inch by inch the teachers and the boys made a garden.

Commencement day in May 1911 found Piney Woods closing its second successful year and ready to go into a busy summer program. Laurence was again heading North with his eyes on a brighter budget for the following year. To avoid a repetition of his ticket-office experience, he sent a messenger several days ahead to pick up his ticket. He also planned to take a good supply of sandwiches—enough to last clear to Iowa if need be.

The students were going home, to help their families with the crops, and taking back to their communities the techniques they had learned during the year. The Yancys planned to stay on at the cabin, to watch the garden and bring in the crops. Doschia Weathersby had, with her principal's help, set up a summer of extension work in which she planned to visit backwoods people, to organize rural improvement groups, cooking classes, corn and poultry clubs among the most isolated farming areas. It was a courageous program for a girl still in her twenties—an itinerary which would mean penetrating on foot the far woods, visiting communities that lay twenty and thirty miles from the nearest railroad. She would have to "find" her food as she went from place to place. But this young woman, just as Laurence and Yancy, felt that Piney

Woods was far more than just a classroom. It was an influence that must be carried out into the farthest corners of the needy area.

On his whirlwind northern tour Laurence was able to raise much more money and get the promise of much more help in less time. On this trip also he personally met Captain Asa Turner, the man who had liked "what you're doing in your corner of the vineyard." It was a quick blossoming of a long and close friendship. "Uncle Asa" promptly pledged a hundred dollars if the colored people of Des Moines would equal it, which they promptly did. He also promised the young teacher that he would come down "and look around" Piney Woods in the near future.

Laurence was back at the school in time for the opening-day services. As he listened to both teachers and students, as they described their summer's activities, he knew that "the spirit of Piney Woods" had begun to catch and inspire.

Doschia Weathersby told about the enthusiasm with which the farm women had greeted her cooking demonstrations and of their husbands' interest in forming clubs for the competitive raising of corn and poultry. Laurence decided that a "Corn Fair" might be a good idea so that the farmers could get together and compare their products at the end of the season.

One girl told about gathering the small children in her neighborhood and teaching them their A B C's. From what he had learned about carpentry at school a boy had built a shed on his father's farm. Another boy told how, by selecting good corn for planting, he had raised ten more bushels an acre than his father and a neighboring farmer on the same kind of land.

Everyone—teachers and students—Laurence realized with a warm sense of gratitude had really tried to do something that summer to improve conditions in their region.

Miss Howland, who had sent the money for the hand press, delighted with the reports that Jones had mailed her, sent a check for the purchase of a larger press so that the school could put out a regular monthly newspaper. Jones immediately bought the press, set it up for operation, and *The Pine Torch* with its slogan, "Give the people light—they will find the way," came into being.

Here was a real opportunity to keep the friends of the school informed as to its activities and progress and, at the same time, to give practical training to the students. Laurence wrote most of the copy, using backwoods sayings and letters from students to lighten his editorials and give the "flavor" of the region. It was not long until he could leave the typesetting and most of the operational work to Georgia Myers and some of the older students.

One of the most obvious needs of the school was for a piano or organ. True, they had song—just as would come from any group of colored folks anywhere—but it could mean so much more if properly accompanied. A few days after school opened Uncle Ed Taylor reported that he had seen a used piano in Jackson that could be bought for $30. Although money was coming in, food and school supplies used it up, and Laurence could not see the justification for spending even this much for the piano.

"Ah likes music," Amon Gibson said, as a group of them were discussing the possibility of buying the instrument, "an' Ah'd like to do something for the school this year, too."

"You've done a lot, Amon," Laurence said. "I don't know what we would have done without your wagon and mules, and you have put in many hours of work also."

"I got me one bale of cotton I been holding," Amon mused. "Mebbe I could take it in and sell it and get that pianner and have a little lef' for my family, too."

"You had better hang on to that cotton yourself," Laurence advised, thinking of the long winter ahead when a family could easily see the bottom of the potato and meal barrels before winter loosed its harsh hand.

The next day Laurence glanced out of the cabin window and saw Amon driving triumphantly into the clearing with the piano in the back of his wagon.

"I got it, 'Fesser, I got the pianner," Amon cried joyfully as Laurence went outside. "They give me $50 fo' my cotton, so I got this and have twenty lef' to go thoo the winter on."

Laurence winced at the thought of how much that money meant to the Gibson family, but Amon did not give him much time to think about it.

"Now," said Amon, "le's get it inside. I wants to hear y'all give some music."

In a jiffy the piano was set up in the chapel, one of the teachers

sat down to play, and a hastily assembled group of students broke
into delighted song. As Laurence looked at Amon's weatherbeaten
face, saw the childish delight as he listened to the notes pour forth,
he hoped that nothing would happen that winter to cause him to
regret his impulsive and generous act.

Six months later Laurence had his answer. " 'Fesser," said Amon,
"I ain't never regretted I bought dat pianner. Of co'se I only got $50
fo' my cotton, but I thought I'd manage somehow, and, you know,
it seems dat since I done dat, money has come to me. I's been able
to git hold of money dat I wouldn't nevah seen if I hadn't done it.
Yep, I'se pow'ful glad I done it!"

Amon was not the only one who figured that anything connected
with Piney Woods School or the "little 'Fesser" would bring good
luck.

As they watched Piney Woods go into its third year, the local
colored people, who had seen this strange institution develop and
grow without "visible means of support," shook their heads in
wonder, and decided it was there to stay. They carried their children dusty miles to deliver them to the "little 'Fesser"; they trailed
him when he walked, and they spoke with hushed awe about this
strange young man who so obviously "had a han'." Just as the
"conjuhs" were influences for the devil, they decided that the
"little 'fesser" and his "mo' dan a mystery" school were powers for
good.

White folks felt the spirit, too—not the black magic of the con-
jurors, but the pleasant tinkle of coin as dark farmers planted good
corn in place of weevily cotton and bought new clothes and furniture, and talked of "mebbe ownin' a piece of lan' " when they got a
little ahead. With such tangible rewards as these the whites were
content to let the "little 'Fesser" throw his magic around most any
which way he cared.

Another happening helped add up to Laurence's growing reputation for white magic. It was enough to have built a school from
"nothin' but prayer" but then, when on stormy days the shuttered
cabin windows allowed scant light and he, with Yancy's help, "cut a
hole in his roof" and glassed it over, that did it. The first skylight in
that part of Mississippi somehow gave the woods folks the notion

that this window in the roof kept the " 'Fesser" in touch with the Boss above.

Laurence was both amused and distressed to find that he had a growing reputation among the Piney Woods people for "havin' a han' " which they thought would help in breaking spells that "debbils and conjuhs" placed on poor folks. He did not know how to dispell this idea. Certainly delivering a talk on the foolishness of superstitions would not do it.

One day, as he worked out in the garden with some of the students, gathering the late fall pumpkins and squash, Laurence looked up to see a strange colored man heading across the garden patch toward him, his face distraught with worry and grief.

"It's mah wife, 'Fesser," gasped the man, who looked as if he had come miles. "I needs he'p. She's done run off and lef' me."

Laurence took him to one side and sat him down. "Tell me about it," he said soothingly.

This was not a new story to him. Some of the wives, Laurence found, had left with another man. Others had merely gone away to a camp meeting or a missionary society and eventually would find their way back.

"She been gone fo' days," the man said.

This looked like a serious case, Laurence decided.

"Yassuh," the man went on, "yassuh, 'Fesser, she sho'ly has. Dat's why I come to you fo' he'p. She's a good woman, 'Fesser, an' she wouldn'ta run off on her own." He turned his wide, worried eyes directly on Laurence, and his voice dropped to a whisper. "Somebody's done *upper-minded her!*"

Laurence promised to do what he could, and then sent the man on his way. He did a bit of inquiring around among people and found out who the woman and her relatives were. He discovered that she had left in a huff, and was merely waiting to cool off. Jones then wrote her, telling her in touching terms of her husband's misery and loneliness and of his desire for her to come home.

A few weeks later Laurence was again in the field when the same man come up to him. It was a changed face—jubilant, happy, thankful. "I know'd you could do it, 'Fesser, I jes' know'd you had a han'." He laughed gleefully. "I know'd you'd take off dat debil's spell, and you did, and she's home."

The man swung a huge sack from his broad shoulders to the ground.

"Dis is all I got now, 'Fesser, jus' a sack of taters. But dey's yours, an' whenever Ah butcher my pig, I'll save you a ham."

As the happy man went jubilantly on his way, Laurence sighed in amazement. Well, there was more than one way to feed the school, it seemed. If he failed at his soliciting, he would just try "his han'."

Chapter 12

A Friend in Deed

From the first time Laurence had walked into John Webster's office he had sensed that this man would be his key figure in his relationship with the local white community. Not only was Webster a man of innate integrity, with a strong sense of justice, but he was also a man of power in the community, the owner of a successful business, and one with which most of the whites had business relationships. His word carried great weight for miles around, even in Jackson. The very fact that Webster had helped the school and was friendly to it caused other men to help also, but, more important, kept many more from hindering.

It was not too much to say, particularly with ex-Governor Vardaman now in the United States Senate, that Webster's calm-eyed, unhysterical support meant the difference between survival and growth—or ashes!

Jones knew, however, that he must widen and strengthen this support both to get more help and to survive. Vardaman had too many followers who devoutly believed that "keeping the nigger ignorant" was the best way to control him.

One crisp windy day in October Laurence received a surprise visit from a Dr. Simmons, one of Jackson's influential citizens, who was in the neighborhood on a medical call.

"Just dropped in to see what is going on," he said.

"I would be pleased to show you what we are doing," Laurence offered.

"Don't mind if you do," the man said, a smile on his jovial face. "It's good to get away from the city."

Laurence immediately sent out students to call a meeting of everyone in the chapel, privately hurried a fast-legged one off to the sawmill to bring John Webster over, and sent others scurrying to other duties.

When the students had assembled, Laurence introduced their guest, who was a bit startled to be among an all-black gathering, seated him on the stage, and then had the students sing spirituals for him. Laurence was greatly relieved when he saw John Webster enter. So was Dr. Simmons. After the two men, who were old acquaintances, shook hands, Laurence said, "I was hoping Mr. Webster could join us for your speech, Doctor."

"A speech, Professah Jones?" Dr. Simmons seemed startled.

"Yes, sir." The winning smile on Laurence's face did not hide its firmness. "We don't have distinguished visitors every day, Dr. Simmons, and our students would appreciate some 'take home' wisdom, some words that they can keep for guidance."

Dr. Simmons glanced from Jones's quiet but insistent face out to the rows of eager-eyed children in front of the stage.

"I think it is a part of education," Professor Jones went on, "for our children to see and meet and listen to guests from the outside— it gives them a broader picture of the world."

"You've said enough, Professah Jones," Dr. Simmons said, obviously flattered. "I'll say a few words."

The good doctor, under the spell of the flattery and the enthusiasm of those eager eyes in front of him, said quite a few words, in fact burst into a flight of oratory which left even himself spellbound. It was a good speech, and when it was over John Webster clasped him warmly by the hand and congratulated him. Laurence smiled his approval. He publicly thanked Dr. Simmons for his message, dismissed chapel, then turned to the two men still seated on the stage.

"Gentlemen," he said, "I want you to have dinner with us."

Dr. Simmons rose from his chair hastily, the joviality on his face turning to fiery anger, and strode off the stage. John Webster was after him in a flash, as Laurence knew he would be.

"Come along, Doctor," he said in his even, persuasive voice, "let's take the Professah up on that offer. I'll bet he feeds us fried chicken!"

Dr. Simmons relaxed, although grave doubt was still reflected in his eyes, and allowed himself to be led to a little room—fortunately prepared just the past week for such an occasion—where there was a neat pine table already set for three. Two girls in fresh white uniforms stood ready to wait on them.

"Be seated, gentlemen," Laurence said.

The two men sat down. Jones motioned to the two girls to begin serving them, which they did, bringing in a huge platter of fried chicken, several dishes of vegetables, and a steaming plate of corn bread—all of which had been especially prepared while chapel services were going on.

John Webster looked up. "Aren't you going to join us, Professah Jones?" he asked.

Laurence glanced at Dr. Simmons, who had his eyes on the platter of chicken.

"Of co'se, Professah Jones," he said.

The conversation was lively, the food was delicious, and few men can part other than friendly when their stomachs are satisfied. Dr. Simmons went his way after expressing his appreciation of the privilege of seeing what was taking place at the school.

Laurence walked part of the way with John Webster toward the sawmill office. As he turned to go back to the school his warm glance showed what was in his heart.

"Thank you, Mr. Webster," he said quietly.

"You're more than welcome," Webster replied with a smile. "Let me know any time you need me. I believe in what you're doin' down there."

"I know you do," Laurence said.

That night at supper big John Webster confided to his wife, "You know, Mother, that fellow Jones is the durndest psychologist that ever hit this part of the country. He can make you do just what he wants you to without even telling you what it is."

"You be careful, John," Mrs. Webster cautioned, her pretty face flushed with concern. "You know what hard things folks around here say about nigger lovers."

"Yes, I know." Webster's jaw set in a sterner line.

The most severe test of John Webster's friendship was not known to Jones for many years. If he had known about it, that winter of 1911, he might not have pursued his work so freely.

Principal Jones was anxious to have men visit his school, men whose word both Northerners and Mississippians would respect and who would both endorse what he was doing and give him ideas on how he could do better. If Piney Woods could bring favorable attention to the community and a stream of northern money into its coffers, everyone would be benefited.

It was a great gratification to him when he received word that "Uncle Asa" Turner was going to make good his promise of the previous summer to come to Mississippi in November for the sole purpose of "looking over" the job that Laurence was doing "in his corner of the vineyard."

Uncle Asa, tall, gaunt, personable, and humanitarian, was a giant in more ways than one. With a fortune amassed late in life, head of the Iowa Corn Growers' Association, and an international reputation on agricultural matters, his interest in and presence at Piney Woods School were something to be pleased about.

One of Jones's first acts, when he found out the exact dates Turner would be there, was to plan Piney Woods' first farmers' conference, to which he invited all of the farmers for miles around, both white and colored. All the students were put to work whitewashing buildings and sheds, to building extra benches, and to getting the diet kitchen in the best possible state of cleanliness and repair. To piece out the meager supply of food students were sent far and near to gather all they could beg or borrow.

The day of Turner's visit fifty white farmers from the Braxton community joined with more than six hundred colored to hear Captain Turner speak. Alive with his subject, Uncle Asa spoke for over an hour on his experiments in corn, on helps in good farming practices, to an absorbed audience. His carefully chosen simple words got over so well that the lowliest torn-coated black farmer there confided later to Jones that he had been "able to foller mos' everythin' he said."

Before and after his speech the students sang spirituals to Uncle Asa's beaming pleasure, and even more so for Amon Gibson's, who never once took his eyes off that "pianner." After the speech dinner was served, with the white folks' nervousness dispelled by John Webster, who grabbed "Coz Caline Barwick," a respected white woman, by the arm and led the way to tables set at one side. Uncle Asa took the seat of honor at the head of the table, gave a rousing blessing in his fine stentorian voice, and dinner was under way.

The next morning Webster found Jones waiting for him at the sawmill office.

"Captain Turner is thinking of writing the Piney Woods School into his will," he said, coming straight to the point, "but he wants to come over and visit with you and get the local reaction first. May I bring him and his wife over to be your guests this afternoon?"

"Of co'se," Webster replied. "I'll be glad to talk to him."

"I have another favor," Laurence went on. "I haven't any means of conveyance at the school in which to bring them. May I borrow your buggy? The captain is too old to walk."

"The buggy's outside," Webster said. "I'll send word to Mrs. Webster to get ready for them. They can spend the night with us."

"Thank you, Mr. Webster."

Laurence hurried out of the office, got in the buggy, and drove to the school.

That afternoon, while it was still daylight, Jones, with Captain and Mrs. Turner beside him in the single-seated buggy, drove to the Websters' house. While the Websters greeted their guests, Laurence carried their bags upstairs to the room where they were to sleep, came back down, and at Webster's suggestion went back to the school in the buggy so that he could pick up the Turners the next day.

The next morning, when he came back for them, he found that the Websters and the Turners had had such a good visit that the Turners had not taken time to pack their bags. While Jones and Webster stood by the buggy waiting, Laurence, as usual, talked of plans for the school. Several men including a mill inspector from Hattiesburg, sixty miles away, a sawmill employee or two, and a few loafers, listened in open-mouthed amazement to his clipped, eager words. Any time he opened his mouth, the teacher was a curiosity to people accustomed to the drawling, hesitant speech of the back-country Negroes. To hear a dark-skinned man "step down on it hard," as they referred to so-called "Yankee" speech, aroused both curiosity and suspicion.

Finally word came that the Turners were packed, and Laurence hustled upstairs to bring down their bags. He put the bags in the back of the buggy, helped the Turners in, then went around and climbed into the driver's seat beside them. They drove off with the

Websters calling out their good-bys. Later in the day Laurence put his guests on the train at Braxton, for their return trip North, left the buggy at the sawmill, and went back to the school, congratulating himself on a most pleasant experience.

The next day John Webster's uncle came to the sawmill office and asked to speak with his nephew alone. Webster sent his secretary and bookkeeper out.

"I come to warn you, John," his uncle said, his eyes troubled, "they're saying hard words about you. I might-a told you you was goin' too far, but you're too bullheaded to listen."

"What do you mean?" Webster asked coldly.

The older man leaned over the desk, his voice dropped to a whisper. "It's about that nigger down at the school. You've got too frien'ly, John."

"Get to the point," Webster said sharply. "What is it they're saying? What have I done?"

"Taken those northern Yankees right into your house," said his uncle.

"You mean the Turners?" Webster gasped in amazement. "Why, weren't you right over at that meeting, too? Don't you know who they are?"

The older man raised a placating hand. "Take it easy, John," he cautioned. "Sure, sure, I know who they are, but they's folks who don't and who don't give a damn—folks say as how you took them damnyankees right into your home, after they'd come from down there at the school where they'd been living with the niggers, and you allowed that nigger to go upstairs in your house, and they allowed him to sit right up beside them in that buggy."

Webster could see it all now. The buggy with only one seat, and the baggage that had to be fetched from upstairs. He and Jones also had stood around talking while they waited for the Turners. He remembered that those men were not local folks, folks that he knew, except that one new sawmill hand.

"What you goin' to do, John?" his uncle asked.

"Nothin' yet," Webster replied.

"You bes' be careful," warned the older man as he left.

For several days John Webster tried to ignore the ugly talk that he knew was floating around, hoping that it would die out. But this was a juicy morsel for gossip in a rural community which lacked excitement. Although the talk had not started with local folks, whom he believed felt kindly toward the school, he knew that it could be taken up by them until it festered into real trouble. He knew that the talk was getting worse by the troubled look in his wife's eyes when he left in the morning, came home to lunch and for the evening.

Finally Webster realized that something must be done to stop it when his storekeeper, Manuel, drew him aside and told him there was talk of getting up a mob to go "whup that nigger good" for his impertinences and then send him, with a good coat of tar and feathers, back "where he belonged." It might even end up, if the spirit of the mob became ugly, in something worse.

Webster strode out of the store to his office where he sent for two of his oldest and most reliable hands, a man named Black and another named George. They both had families, both had sons on the pay roll of the mill, and, more important, they had the confidence of the other workers, who represented a cross section of the community.

Alone with them, he asked them if they had heard about the threats against Jones and his school. They admitted that they had.

"This has got to stop," he said with a finality that left no doubt. "I am going to hold you two responsible for doing it for me. If anything happens to Jones or that school I will shut down this sawmill and personally see to it that every guilty person is arrested or run out of the country. You go back and tell those fellows that I know who they are, and I also know exactly how to reach the federal authorities, if they choose to keep on with their plans."

The would-be troublemakers knew that John Webster meant just what he said. In a few weeks it had all blown over.

When, twenty years later, as the head of an institution in which the entire community took pride, Laurence heard about his narrow escape, he asked Webster why he had not told him about it before.

"I was ashamed for us all," Webster said. "And the only reason I'm telling you now is because it is all past. And besides," his head lifted in a true southern pride, "there wasn't any of the Braxton folks in that, anyway. Nobody that really knew you, or even had had a chance to know you, was in on it. It was outsiders, ignorant outsiders, who had nothin' else to do but stir up a ruckus."

And Jones agreed. He had found that southern men at heart were no different from any others. If given the information, the truth, they would do the right thing. Webster was living, breathing proof of this.

Chapter 13

"Together a Host"

The summer of 1912 Principal Jones once more left a skeleton staff to hold down the school, tend the garden, and continue the extension work in the surrounding country while he headed North. Although he had said nothing to his colleagues about it, he had another serious thought in his mind besides soliciting funds.

Ever since that night in Iowa City, when he had met that "bright little woman" who was raising money for the Kentucky college while he was still an undergraduate, Grace Allen had occupied a special place in his mind. Though he had not seen her since then, he had met no other woman who in any way shadowed his memory of this enthusiastic, charming, and capable teacher. When he had met her he had been a college boy without even a job. Now he was the founder and the principal of a going school that was already attracting wide attention. They had corresponded intermittently through the years and from one of her letters he learned that she was going to spend the summer in Des Moines.

When he met her there Grace Allen proved to be all that Laurence had remembered, and more. A few years older in age and much more in experience than he, this indefatigable woman had already behind her, in addition to her work for the Kentucky institution, a school in Burlington, Iowa, which she had founded single-handed for colored children which had proved so successful that many white families had asked permission to enter their children. When public funds made this school no longer necessary she had gone on to the University of Chicago to take special training in public speaking, preparatory to doing public-relations work. From there she had begun the soliciting work for Eckstein-Norton, which she was doing at the time Laurence first met her and in which she had been extremely successful.

108

Grace Allen was fascinated with everything about the young principal—except his long, long hair, and bushy mustache.

"What on earth made you do that!" she gasped at the first sight of her serious young suitor. "I can't even see you for all that foliage."

Laurence grinned sheepishly, ran a hand over the long "musician's curls" that fell nearly to his shoulders. "There wasn't any other way to make the people listen," he explained.

"You mean to get their attention," bantered Miss Allen, her lively brown eyes glinting with merriment. "They probably stood around in shocked silence." She sighed with mock sadness. "And I remembered you as a rather handsome young man."

"Give me a couple more good years, with a few more buildings, and maybe I can afford to come clean," Laurence said. "But not now."

With the big job that lay ahead, the couple saw no reason to wait, and they were married in Des Moines, honeymooned briefly in Minnesota, then Laurence left his bride with his mother, who was now living in Marshalltown, and went valiantly back at his job of raising money.

Finding such a partner to help with his work at Piney Woods was for the "little 'Fesser" a stroke of unbelievably good fortune. A woman of indomitable energy, she was equipped to teach English, sewing, handcrafts, a competent office worker, and an expert at raising money. Above all, she was fascinated with the job he was doing in the Black Belt.

That fall, on opening day of the fourth year of Piney Woods School, October 21, 1912, when the students and the farmers gathered at the grounds for the services, without any preliminary warning Laurence appeared before them with Grace by his side.

As he introduced her a gasp of astonishment, a wave of curious whispers, and a spontaneous craning of necks took place as the simple-hearted country folk sought to see for themselves just what their "little 'Fesser" had "done fo' hisself."

Laurence led the audience in the Lord's Prayer, then called upon the teachers and students to make their reports, while he sat beside his wife.

Though Piney Woods, in this its fourth year of existence, had as yet no graduates, its influence was being felt far and wide. Boys told of work in fields in which they applied new techniques, girls spoke of teaching younger children both how to read and write and also how to cook, both boys and girls told of organizing Sunday-school classes. Several mentioned saving and collecting a few pennies here and there to start a school band—one of the many dreams that Laurence had for the school.

Then the parents spoke. The farmers told of still another discouraging year—the third successive season of crop failure due to the boll weevil and heavy rains. The old story which meant no money for tuition for their children. It would be up to them, with what little in the way of animals and produce and poultry that could be spared, to work their way.

Teachers, students, parents—all spoke, but the collective eye of the audience for once was not on their "little 'Fesser" but on the small, mobile-faced woman who sat so quietly but who listened with such intensity to what was said.

When they had all finished Laurence rose, congratulated the teachers and the students on a job well done, and then tried to encourage the farmers and their wives by telling them that other farm communities had survived scourges and plagues of the same sort by working out methods to combat them, and that one of the projects of the school would be to get the latest information on what to do about the boll weevil and make it available to them. He also announced another farmers' conference at the school like the one that had been given when Uncle Asa Turner had visited them, and that he would get the best speaker to talk with them that he could persuade to come. Then he called upon his wife to say a few words.

Grace Jones rose, bowed a warm acknowledgment to the polite applause that greeted her, and then began to speak. She had a message of hope and encouragement that went right to the hearts of her listeners. Furthermore, she had plans which she had been working on since the day of her marriage, and she launched into them with heartening enthusiasm.

As the excited throng marched to dinner, after the services, an old man caught Laurence by the arm. " 'Fesser," he said, "we all thought dat you was de bes' man and de bes' talker dat we all evah seed, but since we has met vo' old lady and heered her, we's decided dat you has gone an' beat yo'se'f!'"

An old woman was even more forthright. She told him that the women had been worried when he first appeared with his new wife. " 'Fesser," she said in a voice deep with emotion, "we all loves you, and we been prayin' for you, but we was afeared dat you might go an' bring back some hifalutin' gal dat wouldn't notice us poor folks." She sighed with heartfelt relief. "We is all so glad *you has did well!*"

With their direct pipeline to nature, uncomplicated by the over-lardings of sophistication, these country folk looked straight at the " 'fesser's gal" and liked what they saw. Despite her different back-ground and their lack of education, Grace Jones at once fitted into the Piney Woods community—a rapport possible through a sincere concern and dedication to helping those whose life "started at a discount." She did this in spite of a distinct shock. Although she had listened with eager attention to all her young husband had told her of the backwoods of Mississippi, what she had heard had not quite prepared her for what she saw in that sea of black faces that were turned toward her with a light of hope.

But she was to see more. All day long students appeared, toiling up the paths and trails, with their belongings tied in bandanas and "all the superstitions and ignorances of their backward communi-ties" held fast in their heads. But they had come to "get eddicated."

One widow, the mother of twelve children, appeared with her oldest girl, to find out if she could be entered "withouten money." They had walked more than twelve miles "just to see."

One farmer unloaded a squealing pig from a wagon. He had brought his seventeen-year-old son, crippled by an accident with an ax, to be "eddicated" because "he warn't much good fer farmin'." His one chance to earn a living lay in learning a trade.

Children, children, children. Orphans, half-orphans, children of slaves, children of broken homes, children who had never seen a railroad or a train. Children on foot, in wagons, children with their parents, and children alone.

The story was always the same—a terrible crop year—no money for tuition. A load of hay for one girl; two dozen jars of preserves for another; four live geese for a third. But for the majority there was nothing.

"How many can we take?" Grace asked her husband.

"We have room for only eighty-five boarders, but perhaps we can squeeze in a hundred," Laurence decided. "Then we will take as many day students as we can possibly handle."

Day students! The children who were no more than five or six miles away. Barefoot black youngsters sturdy enough to walk. Many of them in the past years had not missed a day. When the weather was freezing, or shoes could not be found for them, they wrapped their feet in burlap and came anyway.

One girl, whose mother was dead and who had five younger children to look after, set herself a schedule (and kept it) for the year: "Stay home weekends and cook and clean for the week ahead, then walk seven miles to Piney Woods, room with some relatives that lived nearby during the week, then walk the seven miles home on Friday night, to clean, cook, wash, and scrub to last the next week."

As Mrs. Jones made such notations, she realized, as Laurence had told her, how heartbreaking it was to turn anyone down. Better to squeeze a little more, better to do without space that might mean the difference between being crowded and comfort.

When the opening day was finally over and the older people had gone back to their homes—with brighter spirits than they had come—and the "bride and groom" sat before a pine-knot fire in a room partitioned off in the little cabin which was their first home, Grace Jones put down the pencil with which she had been making notes of immediate needs and stared thoughtfully into the fire.

"I suppose I knew from what you had told me," she said slowly, "that it would be heartbreaking. But somehow I didn't quite realize there would be so many and so pitifully poor." She looked at her husband, who was sitting at his desk busily preparing copy for *The Pine Torch*. "How many children are there in this area, children for whom Piney Woods School is the only real educational facility?"

Laurence looked across at his wife with a half-sad smile. "Eleven thousand, two hundred and fifty," he said.

"Eleven thousand, two hundred and fifty!" Grace echoed. "And we have room—for a hundred!"

"When we started three years ago we didn't have room for ten," Laurence reminded her.

"I know," murmured his wife, her wide eyes still fixed on the glowing logs. "If you had hunted the world over, you couldn't have picked a spot where a job was more needed." She smiled, her face alight with purpose. "What a place to dedicate your life!"

The next day, when classes officially began at Piney Woods, there was an enrollment of one hundred sixty-nine students and a staff of eight teachers, the newest of whom, Grace Jones, absorbed the bulk of the English classes as well as the supervision and directing of a handcrafts department—something that had been on Principal Jones's mind for a long time. In addition she headed the extension work which she intended to carry on throughout the year as well as during the summer term.

The Braxton community, deeply impressed by what was happening, primarily through the generosity of Webster, Mangum, Everett, and Cox, came forward with the offer of a dormitory for the girls, and in a short time Braxton Hall, with facilities for housing forty girls, was added to the physical plant. In addition, from the lumber that was left over the teachers and students built a one-room manual-training shop.

Not to be outdone, the poor farmers who lived nearby, with no money but with a lot of enthusiasm, cut enough timber out of the pine forests to build a little log cabin for a blacksmith shop and one in which to make brooms.

The trouble was that, with the place taking on the looks of a real school campus, more and more students applied for admission.

"We must have buildings—more and more buildings," Grace Jones decided.

"It's taken all I could raise each summer to keep us in food through the year," her husband said.

"It'll be different next year," she promised. "We'll both go out in the summer. With both of us working all summer, we should raise at least twice as much, shouldn't we?"

"We should," Laurence agreed, pleased at the glow of determination on his wife's face. "We can't turn any of these children down, can we?"

"No," said Grace solemnly. "Not so long as we have the physical strength to help them."

Besides their regular classes, the Piney Woods teachers carried on what they called "settlement work" during the year. Both Mr.

and Mrs. Jones prepared questionnaires which they sent out over the countryside with such questions as:

What improvements have you made on your house in the past five years?

What have you done to improve your children's minds?

"I went by the field of the slothful and by the vineyard of the man void of understanding and lo, it was all grown over with thorns and nettles had covered the face thereof and the stone wall was broken down."

WAS IT YOUR PLACE?

When she was not teaching classes, Mrs. Jones went out into the community, working with local women, organizing sewing, cooking, and canning groups, and giving home and group instruction in these activities. With her help Laurence brought off his farmers' conference and his corn show, both of which were enthusiastically attended.

Local women were invited to join the canning, sewing, and handcraft classes at the school. The classrooms were crowded—as were the shops—with eager learners from boys of ten up to men of fifty and sixty. Sometimes the local men actually enrolled in the classes; others just "drapped by" to pick up what information they could in an hour or so.

Amon Gibson appeared almost every day not to attend classes but just to be in contact with his young friend. They might sit for a chat on the log under the old cedar tree, which had grown a bit of a top since the tornado, or he might plump down on a bench near Laurence's desk, to ask, " 'Fesser, where'd the boll weevil come from?" or what did the Lord mean by some quotation from the Bible. And always those gray mules, which lived up to their reputation by not dying, and that sturdy wagon was at the disposal of the school for any hauling needs.

Mrs. Gibson, who did day work for the white folks at Braxton, made tremulous reports to her husband of the fact that "Crazy" Jones was still talked about, and sometimes some of them talked "hard" of him, but most of them, the good men like Mr. Mangum or Mr. Webster or Mr. Cox, "why dey would perk right up and say, 'now you leave that nigger be. You jus' wait till he makes a misstep befo' you start talkin'.' " And the white ladies, "soon as dey got to know Missus Jones, why dey started takin' right up fer her in front of ev'body."

Grace Jones, from the beginning, had realized the wisdom of her husband's approach to the white world with which they had to live. Sharing his innate love for the "whole human race" it was not difficult for her to accept, with gracious forbearance, the inbred prejudices of the community and show her good will by acts of kindness and neighborliness. She, too, could "inch her way" along toward a better day and could help prepare for it as she went.

During an influenza epidemic which swept the community that winter, white and colored, with devastating swiftness, everyone at the school jumped in with a hearty good will to help out. Amon Gibson's wagon went all over the community with food already prepared to be distributed where no one was well enough to cook and with medicines when available. Both teachers and students went from house to house, nursing, cheering up the sick, and doing all manners of household and outside work. At Christmastime groups of singers toured the homes of the crippled and sick and sang carols for them.

This was a kind of good will that could not be overlooked. The kind of human warmth against which there is no defense. More and more the word spread from person to person, and house to house, to "leave that nigger alone." In a way it was a command, a sort of community sentiment, and yet the going was and would still be "touchy."

Along toward spring, when Piney Woods had scheduled a concert for a Friday evening, a half-hour before it took place Laurence was startled when a white man, a Mr. Barwick from Braxton, suddenly appeared at the school grounds wearing a brace of six-shooters.

"What is wrong? What has happened?" Laurence asked.

"Nothing yet," said Barwick grimly, taking a sturdy-legged stand near the chapel door, where the light would fall on him. "I heard there was some old rowdy white boys was a-goin' to get likkered up an' come down here and break up you-all's concert. An' I just wanted to stand here where I could *discourage* 'em a little!"

Yes, Laurence remembered, Grace had helped nurse Barwick's wife a month or so before. He sincerely hoped that nothing would

happen, but it was also reassuring that that stern-faced man felt the
way he did about it.

The concert went off without a hitch, with the white folks enjoy-
ing it as much as the colored. Whether the boys had been "discour-
aged" before they started, or whether the sight of Barwick with his
"artillery" did the trick, Laurence never found out.

As the days went on Laurence, with Grace's help, concentrated
more and more upon bringing to the attention of both the students
in the school and all of the colored inhabitants of the community the
necessity for a sense of time and for dependability. Slavery certainly
had done everything to discourage these attributes.

As one student later said, "He taught us how to do ordinary things
in an extraordinary way." Each student made out a daily report sheet
which was turned into the principal at the end of the day:

> Who started work later than 7 A.M?
> Who quit before twelve?
> Who lost time during the day? Why?
> What did you accomplish today?

It was a hard life at Piney Woods, a life which could provoke
legitimate grumbling which, after all, did no harm—the "rising"
bell rang at 5 A.M. and there was half a day's work—hard manual
work—of clearing fields and woods, planting, harvesting, sewing,
cooking, serving, washing, all with the most meager equipment.
Then there was half a day of classes, and additional classes at night
for those who worked their way in full. Another bell at nine forty-
five announced that it was time to go to bed for the healthy sleep
that would mean the strength for a repetition of the same program.

For the benefit of students who worked during the day and
attended school only at night, the warning supper bell—their signal
to quit work in the afternoon—was rung half an hour earlier "during
the darkest days of winter."

Not much of a concession that, but Principal Jones made few,
and his wife agreed wholeheartedly in the rigor of the program. It
was necessary not only because of the meager resources of the school
but because of the background of the students. "We colored folks
allus spoil our chillun," one woman said, in defense of their laziness,

"but 'Fesser, he don't do dat. He teaches 'em to toe de mark—be on time and work hard an' nevah idle. He teaches 'em how to get ahead."

Others grumbled when they found that they worked twice as hard at school as they had at their homes. But the steadfast workers far outweighed the grumblers, and there was always before them the example of the teachers from Jones on down who worked not hours but until they "got finished," which seemingly was never.

The following spring Jones, with the help of Grace, prepared a brochure to be sent out both to the people in the neighborhood and to the friends of the school in the North. Among some of the pertinent questions were these:

"Do you want an education or would you rather remain ignorant? An ignorant black laborer or a colored citizen?

"You can never again say, 'I did not have a chance.' This is your chance.

"We accept yearlings, chickens, hogs, and farm produce the same as cash money," said the brochure.

"If a student brings a cow or a colt, it will pay for a year's schooling—or more."

Piney Woods closed the school year of 1912—1913 with a financial statement prepared by Wiley Mangum at the Braxton bank. It showed that the school had taken in $3,370 during the year and had spent $3,720, $2,220 of which had gone into permanent improvements. The expense for teachers, eight of them including Principal Jones, for the year had been $360.53. Cash on hand was— NONE.

But they had a "capital asset" far more valuable than cash. One of the teachers expressed it this way, "Taken separately, Mr. and Mrs. Jones are almost superhuman; together they are a host."

On a second visit to Piney Woods Captain Asa Turner reported, "They have the confidence of the best white people around them and the entire support of the colored people—only they are so pitiably poor. Yet they are taking hold with rare courage. The little faculty is serving without adequate pay and they are all surely building their lives into the work."

Another visitor, Dr. J. D. Harris, brother of N. W. Harris, the founder of the Harris Bank and Trust Company of Chicago, wrote to his Illinois home-town newspaper that "A farmer in a wagon drove into the school the day I was there, with his daughter and six gallons of cane syrup with which to enter her!" Then, after a description of the campus, which he found "severely plain, not to say crude," Dr. Harris concluded, "I know of no work where a dollar will go further in effecting an uplift of a people, white or black, than in this work that is being done at Piney Woods School."

This sort of support sent Laurence and Grace northward when summer came with lighter hearts and a more dedicated purpose.

Chapter 14

"Inchin' Along"

Three crude two-story pine buildings, a cluster of six smaller ones, all tucked in a clearing on the side of a hill, a big barn that was being built from money the Joneses had raised during the summer—this was Piney Woods School in the fall of 1913. Oil lamps and wood stoves for cooking, fireplaces for heating, a spring-house from which water was "toted" by hand, no school desks for the students except rough, half-finished benches on which they put their books and writing tablets, then squatted on the floor to write, leading one visitor to think she had "accidentally stumbled into a Bible class and they were all praying." But there was money enough to run the school for the year with "almost enough to eat" and "almost enough blankets" to keep warm. Grace Jones had made good her promise to double the amount collected the previous summer. They had actually done a little better.

Looking at it in some ways, as Professor Linaeus Weld, dean of the College of Liberal Arts at the University of Iowa remarked after a visit, it was "pitiably inadequate." But looking at it in another way, as he also said, "There is a definiteness and strength of purpose, an adaptation of simple means to practical ends, an enthusiasm on the part of pupils and teachers, and certainty of reasonable success in their work, which even the most favored of our colleges could afford to sacrifice much to secure."

Looking back, five years, to its inception, Piney Woods was truly "mo' dan a mystery" to the band of faithful "children of the soil" who had seen it grow literally right out of the ground before their eyes. When Mrs. Jones, who had returned first from the North, announced that the "little 'Fesser" would be back for the opening day of the fifth term, country folks gathered from far back in the woods to welcome him. This was a special welcome, a different welcome. Perhaps due to the additional stability which his marriage had given, perhaps the constantly increasing number of buildings, it was as if word had been passed, from farm to farm, from settlement to settlement, that "Piney Woods is here to stay. And today we will celebrate."

They were there, hundreds of them, on opening day, and as Principal Jones came before them to speak, he felt the flavor of the meeting, the odd spirit which banded them together. It was as if before they had not really quite believed, but that now they did, and that no longer, like a beckoning mirage, this "miracle" might vanish before their eyes. They were here, this time, really to celebrate its existence. It had stood the trial of the "borning" period. Now it was a permanent part of the community.

"Today marks the beginning of the fifth year of this little school," Jones said. "In the glow of a bonfire five years ago, before we had adequate shelter, I saw many of your faces light up with a new understanding of the meaning of education as we studied our books and practiced our manual training. A song you have just finished typifies the spirit of this institution more than anything I know. Well may we sing

> "Keep a-inchin' along
> Jesus will come by and by,

which came out of the hearts of our foreparents in the dark days of slavery, for even today we need such a sentiment to guide us over the rugged road we must travel if we are to reach success."

Then, as his glance swept over many familiar faces in the crowd, people who had come from deep back in the woods, he called upon them to give their "testimony" as to what the school had meant to them.

First, Rease Berry moved forward. " 'Fesser," he said, "us colored folks have been startin' up projects of one kind and another ever since de war—schools, cotton gins, an' lots of other things, I don't know what all. But we'd always fall out and bust it up 'cause every feller wanted to be de leader." He smiled gratefully at Jones. "This school jus' beats eve'thing."

Next, Oscar Cox, one of the farmers who had helped on the

original building, took the floor. "I'm glad we's spared to meet here again," he said, "fo' dis year we's got a chance to do a whole lot better dan evah befo'. I wants my chillun and dese other chillun to do a whole lot better and learn a heap—'cause 'fesser sure has brought in a fine crop of teachers."

As each speaker took his seat, Laurence no longer had to point out the one who was to speak. Another rose, as though compelled by the emotion of the moment, to voice his thoughts. As Oscar Cox sat down, Jems McLaurin got up. "I remember," he said, "when dese grounds was jus' a woods an' an ole fiel' "—he gestured to include the whole stretch of campus land—"but the powah of education has changed it!" A smile spread over his dark face as he thought of that "powah" and then his face saddened slightly. "I'se only sorry dat I haven't taken advantage of it mahself, but I have given my chilluns de chance."

Then Rhodes McDonald, who had come from his home fourteen miles in the woods. "I'm pleased to see de community pleased. There's gen'ally someone to throw a stumblin' block in de way. Dis school has meant an improvement to us colored folks. I want to tell you what my boy done. His grandma give him nine jints of cane. Well, de fus' year he got seven stalks, an' saved de eyes an' kep' right on plantin' and sellin' until he's been able to buy him a yoke of oxen from dem nine jints!"

Mrs. Ed Taylor got up to remind " 'Fesser Jones" what a real helper he had gotten for himself when he married Mrs. Jones. "Why, things are carried on now like dey never was befo'," she concluded.

Taking courage from Mrs. Taylor's lead, Mrs. Janie Barber rose next. "I jes' want to let you know, 'Fesser, I'm a-prayin' for you. I prays fo' you an' Miz Jones, for dat good white woman who gave dat printin' press, for Uncle Asa Turner, and for all dat have done so much."

Next, Please Williams, a dark giant of a man with a warm, glistening smile, loomed before the crowd. He started to speak, shook his head with a rich, booming laugh, and started again: "I'm jes' too full to 'spress mahself," he admitted in a choking voice. "Many times I has got on my knees and talk to God about helping dis place to go on. Say"—once more he shook his head as if to shake out the confusion—"I jes' can't say nothin'. Others have fixed it up good with dere talkin' and if I go on in mah ignorant way you'll forget all de good things dey said." He sat down to a wave of warm laughter and applause.

But the laughter was only a momentary release from the spirit that gripped them all. Now Mrs. McGee was standing, her head thrown back to reveal the taut lines of her face, the strong light that burned in her eyes. "It was five years ago," she began, her voice tense with emotion, "dat I fus' heard of dis school. I was livin' back in de country—forty or fifty miles from hyear. One of de teachers came by an' told me about it. Well, I didn't see how we could ever git to it, as we was poor an' have a large family. But"—her luminous eyes swept the crowd—"I want to tell you, *I went down the knee way,* I trusted God, I prayed He would help to obtain de blessing of school for my chilluns. And now, praise de Lord, we are right hyear in de neighborhood. Dat's why I trust in God! I want to tell you all, *God must be in dis place.* His words are revealed. My! but I'm happy! De Lord has provided a way for my chilluns."

As she built up to the peak of her emotions, Mrs. McGee's voice reached a vibrant crescendo, and as she finished, she sank back into her place. An old woman in the crowd who had been a slave burst out in an eerie, unintelligible spiritual, which ended in a wild chant.

As Principal Jones once more took the floor, to make an announcement, Mrs. Ed Taylor rose to her feet.

"Please excuse me, 'Fesser," she said, "but I'm 'roused! You have done my heart good. De Lord has answered my prayers." As if one, the vast black crowd in unison murmured, "Amen."

It was a strange, moving spectacle, with all of the elements of a revival meeting. Thanks and prayers and raw emotions and deep gratitude to the Lord and the man who had made a dream come true. As he looked at them, and realized what it meant in terms of hope and emotion, the "little 'Fesser" felt a load of heavy responsibility descend upon him, and he pledged himself that, if possible, he must make certain that whatever happened to him nothing must happen to destroy this fulfillment of a dream.

"It isn't just your school any more," Grace said to him as they talked over what should be done after the crowd had left. "As of today it is an institution belonging to these people."

"I know," Laurence answered, "it's big enough now and important enough to the community that it's really more than one person should handle."

"Do you think we could get a charter from the state and set up a regular board of trustees to run it?" Grace asked.

"That is what we must have," Laurence replied, "but I don't know how many men around here would jeopardize their positions to sign a petition for us. After all, it would be asking a lot from our friends with the feeling that exists." He was thinking about the constant turmoil which Vardaman and others were keeping at the boiling point.

"To be associated with any cause for the betterment of the colored race is certainly political suicide," Grace admitted, "but don't you think fair-minded businessmen—men like Mr. Mangum and Mr. Everett over at the bank and Major Millsaps at Jackson who has always spoken up for the school—would be willing to go with us."

"Yes, and we could have our own people sign it—Uncle Ed and Amon and Hector McLaurin," Laurence mused. "Perhaps you are right about the other three. I don't want to ask John Webster. He has done more than enough already. Then we could get a couple of men from the North."

"We would want Uncle Asa," Grace said.

"I think Dr. Harris would be willing to serve," Laurence said. "He seemed quite interested in what happens here."

So the charter was drawn up with three local colored men, two northerners, and the three southern white men.

One of the hardest things Laurence ever did was to ask these southern white men to put their names on the charter. It was one thing privately to support a position so unpopular as Negro education and quite another to go on public record. But he found to his great pleasure when he approached them that they not only agreed to serve on his board but actually seemed flattered that he had asked them.

"I think that in all the world," Jones later wrote, "there has never been a group of braver men than those formally behind our effort."

The charter was duly drawn, signed, and submitted to the governor of Mississippi, and on May 17, 1913, "The Piney Woods Country Life School" legally and formally came into existence. "The purpose for which it is created is to establish, maintain, and develop a country-life school in which to train the head, heart, and hands of colored boys and girls for a life of Christianity, character, and service." It was further stipulated that "the cost of education shall, as far as practicable, be reduced to the lowest point consistent with the efficient operation of said school and every reasonable effort shall be made to bring education for country life within the ability of the poor classes of the Black Belt. . . ."

Thus 1913 was a turning point for Piney Woods—from an "experiment" into a durable institution with corporate life—just as the woods folks had sensed intuitively when they gathered to welcome the "little 'Fesser" on opening day the fall before.

News of the school and its progress was reaching all corners of the country. A steady stream of visitors came to see it from the North, resulting in more and more contributions for books and food. The school garden was aiding materially in feeding the students, though the diet was still basically the cowpeas, greens, and corn bread of former days. It was, however, occasionally spiced with home-canned vegetables and fruits and some fresh meat. As the "little 'Fesser" himself admitted, he was not so apt to just ";drop in" on neighboring friends around mealtime and "protestingly" accept of their invitation to "set up" to the table with them.

The first white teacher came to Piney Woods in 1913. Mrs. Nellie Brooks, an ex-teacher from Waterloo, Iowa, who had been a stalwart in helping them raise money, became so fascinated with the activities down in Mississippi that she moved in, bag and baggage, to teach "for free" and to become actively associated with this humanitarian program.

The announced arrival of Mrs. Brooks presented a frightening problem. Privations were one thing to laugh over in airy discussion in comfortable surroundings, quite another to put up with in daily living. Grace and Laurence thought of Mrs. Brooks's well-furnished, well-appointed, and comfortable house in Waterloo, and shook their heads as they considered their own partitioned-off corner of the cabin.

There was a great flurry and scurry of board splitting, of building, and of whitewashing. By the time their friend arrived for her stay at Piney Woods the students had built a little cabin for her—

of freshly cut forest pine, quite charming in its rustic simplicity if
not in its comforts.

Mrs. Brooks was delighted and moved in with a small store of
treasures she had brought along—books and curtains and pictures
that helped lend the interior some of her own fastidious and feminine
personality. She enjoyed teaching the wide-eyed dark children, loved
their fascination with her and her house. And all was fine until the
rains set in and the cabin, like all the other "student-constructed"
buildings, leaked around every log. Mrs. Brooks, however, despite
her gentle background, stayed on, and ended up by staying two full
years at Piney Woods for which she received no pay. She was the
first of a series of warmhearted folk who, drawn by the amazing
spirit of Piney Woods, were to come and offer their services for a
chance to participate in such a Christian and democratic institution.

Of the ladylike and charming Mrs. Brooks one country woman
reported that her son, who was "mos' nigh" ten years old, volun-
teered, for the first time, to wash his face on the day that he "was
goin' to work for Miz Brooks." For such devotion a few privations
were worth enduring.

The following summer Principal and Mrs. Jones signed up for a
tour of the Redpath Chautauqua Circuit with its opportunity for
carrying the story of their school through the North. "It will give
us enough money to pay for food and school supplies next year,"
Laurence said.

"And perhaps enough extra to build another building so we can
take more students," Grace added.

While in Des Moines, Laurence had an unbelievable stroke of
good fortune. One of his Iowa University classmates, W. O. Fink-
bine, came to see him.

"Laurence," he said, "my brother and I own eight hundred acres
of land down your way and we looked up to see, and blamed if it
isn't right next to your school. It's cut-over timberland but I imagine
you could use it."

Use it! Room to spread out on, room to farm, an adequate supply
of firewood for years to come. This was one of the most promising
gifts the school had ever received.

With this exciting sendoff the summer tour was a resounding
success. At the same time, it was shadowed by the old bugaboos of

travel—the denial of restrooms, the trouble getting tickets; the refusal of food and hotel service, humiliations and privations which were individually hard enough to endure but acutely painful to the young teacher now that he must share them with the educated and sensitive woman who was his wife.

Yet, though their experiences were doubly galling to Laurence, Grace moved through them all with a quiet dignity which usually left the oppressor the flustered one.

There were nights when Laurence was glad she was not with him, once when he had to spend the night in a boxcar and another spent in jail after a demoralizing "vagrancy" arrest by an overzealous policeman who thought all people of color should carry passports after dark. And this was the North.

But ranged against these thoughtless and ignorant acts were the kind friends. As they traveled the Joneses gradually built up a circle of acquaintances whose "homes were their homes" whenever they were in their parts of the country, and who insisted they plan their itineraries so they would spend nights with them rather than face hotel and rooming-house embarrassment.

Years later the mayor of a large northern city, a man with a "deep South" background, told a white teacher from Piney Woods how Mrs. Jones had come to see him and later he had found out that, for the want of a place to sleep, she had been forced to spend the night with a "woman of questionable reputation" in the poorest section of his city because she had been refused a room everywhere else.

"It made me positively ill," said the mayor, "when I thought of a charming, dignified little lady like that forced to such extremes. I decided right then and there that whenever she came again I would insist she be my guest in my house."

Bit by bit the circle was forged. If one had the patience and the farsightedness to survive the rough edges, there must be a smoother rim ahead long enough to catch the breath for the next struggle.

Chapter 15

"De Lord's Laid His Hands on Me"

"Did you ever see the like before?
Oh, I know de Lord's laid his hands on me . . ."

The first clouds of the United States' possible entry into World War I hung over America in early 1917, filtering even into the consciousness of backwoods folks, when a minister friend of Jones's in a nearby state west of Mississippi asked him to help conduct a revival meeting. Although Jones was not a preacher, his fame in arousing farming communities to a more thrifty and industrious life had spread through the South, and this minister felt that having his practical words added to the religious revival would both draw and inspire the farm folks.

Though overworked at Piney Woods, Jones felt that he must accept this invitation since it gave him a chance to reach a wider audience quite as needy as the group with which he daily worked.

The first day of the revival, at the time of his initial address, the little country church bulged with colored people.

"Life is a battleground," he told them, drawing his analogies from military life. "We must stay on the firing line and wage constant battle against ignorance, against superstition, against poverty. We must marshal our faith. . . ."

As his militant words lashed out in clear-cut, clipped speech, to and over the heads of his audience, and out of the open doors and windows into the calm, country air, a pair of idle white farm boys, ambling by on horseback, heard them. They checked their horses and drew close enough to the church to peer in the door and catch phrases of Jones's speech, phrases such as "firing line," "wage battle," and "keep fighting"—phrases out of context which to their war-excited, ignorant young minds spelled only one thing—the

thing which race-baiters such as Vardaman, as well as the German
agents working in America in 1917, had been propagandizing: "If
the United States goes to war, the Negroes will rise up and revolt."
The boys spurred their horses toward their homes, spreading the
word as they tore along: "Speaker up t' church is urging all the
niggers to rise up and fight the white people."

Next morning, as the second session of the revival meeting got
under way, there was a commotion outside and the congregation and
its guest speaker looked out to see a band of fifty white men forming
a circle around the church.

A frightening silence fell over the congregation. Laurence glanced
from the stormy-faced men who appeared at the door to the little
black band of worshipers inside, their eyes blanched gray, a piteous,
knowing fear in their eyes.

"Come outside," barked the leader, pointing at Laurence as the
two boys beside him identified their quarry.

A sweeping sigh, like the whispering death of leaves, echoed
Laurence's footfalls as he walked down the aisle toward the door.
The leader and the boys fell back as he reached them, then closed
in behind him. Someone threw a rope over his head, drew up the
noose, and pulled it forward.

Laurence found himself marching down the road in the center of
an armed guard. A strange nightmarish numbness seized him as his
feet obediently followed one after the other. The faces of the men
around him seemed to have melted into an angry jumble, devoid
of all humanity. No words were said as they moved forward; only
the tromp of the feet of the men immediately circling him and the
hoofbeats from the mounted outer circle broke the deathly silence.

As he walked, there streamed through Laurence's head a phantom
strain of disconnected melody—fragments of the old songs of trouble
and death. It was as if, during those last, lost moments he was carrying on his own back the sadness and the agony of his race. *Mary,
don't you weep, don't you mourn. . . . Were you there when they
nailed Him to the tree? Do, Lord, remember me! When I'm in trouble, when I'm dying, why this earth's on fire, do, Lord, do, Lord,
remember me! . . .* And out of his childhood old Aunt Liza's haunting
query:

"An' am I a-borned to die?
To a-lay this body down?"

And louder than all, his father's cry of impotent agony: "What if they lynches a black man every day! How long is Old Glory going to be the covering of a cussed thing like that?"

Then he realized the band had stopped its march. He looked before him with history-drenched eyes. They had come to a clearing. A giant tree stood in the center and from it stuck out, as an accusing finger, a single jagged limb. Beneath it was piled a mound of brush, ready for the match.

Around the edge of the clearing a throng of men and boys had gathered, and more streamed in from all sides. As the "guard" led their culprit forward, two teenage boys let out wild animal cries and shinnied up the tree to help get the rope over the limb.

When the vast crowd had formed a circle around him, Laurence looked out over the unending sea of human faces and saw but one conglomerate face from which mass hatred had momentarily drained human mercy. Four of the strongest men lifted him and tossed him up on the brush pile. As his slight body sailed through the air a roar broke from the throats of the mob. A scattering of shots rent the air as men tested their guns to be certain they were ready in case their prisoner attempted to run. The rope, with the help of the boys, was thrown over the limb.

Laurence pulled himself up so that he could get a footing on the pyre, then stood facing the mob, waiting for the rope to tighten and the flick of fire at his feet.

Before his eyes flashed the faces of his wife, the teachers, his southern white friends, and the simple, trusting piney woods folk and their eager-eyed children who were his "children," too—the ones he had tried to help. Then he glanced at this sea of faces before him now, devoid of justice, and he felt sick for the whole human race.

And then a strange thing happened. One man, caught either by that fate-filled face before him or merely driven by a desire to prolong the excitement, jumped up on the pyre beside him and waved his hat for silence.

"I want to hear him make a speech befo' we string him up," he said.

"Yeah, let him talk." "Let's have a speech." "Tell us what you told them niggers yesterday!"

"Yes, I'll make you a speech," Laurence cried quickly before the mass mind should shift. "I'll tell you what I told them!"

Balanced firmly on his pile of brush, with the rope slack around his throat, Laurence started talking—talking as he had never talked before—strong, clean words that cut sharply but simply across the curious silence. Humble words but not begging ones. He spoke of the South of both the Negro and the white, the land where they all lived and must keep on living together. He told about his school, about what he was trying to do to make that living together easier for both white and black. He told them of the many southern white men who had learned to trust him and who had helped him. He called names that some of them there knew. He repeated what he had said the day before and just what he had meant by it. He explained that they were all caught in "a battle of life," just as this country might be forced to fight the German effort to enslave the whole world, that the fight he was putting up was against superstition, against poverty, and particularly against ignorance. He even wooed them to laughter, giving them a moment's respite in which to relax before he hit again—at the message they must learn if their beloved land was to survive and be more than an ugly battleground of hates. And then at last when he felt he could let go, when there was nothing more to say, he concluded with this solemn statement: "There is not a man standing here who wants to go to his God with the blood of an innocent man on his hands."

Then he waited before them, quiet once more.

There had been noise and interruption as he spoke—laughter, some shouts, some heckling, and every once in a while a clap of hands. But as he finished a great shout went up, shouts and roars of approbation, as the men, as though released from a spell, looked guiltily at each other.

Suddenly an old man, wearing a tattered Confederate army coat, pushed his way through the crowd. Scrambling up beside Laurence on the brush pyre, he reached over and with gentle hands lifted the noose from his neck.

"Come on down, boy," he said. "We jes' made a slight mistake."

Men came forward and slapped Laurence on the shoulder as he climbed down; others strode up with outstretched hands.

Far back in the crowd a disappointed murmur went up, mostly from younger men, as they realized they were going to miss the fun. But the real danger was over. The older and solider members of the mob had been reached somehow through the power of words; the appeal to their innate sense of justice.

"Let's help the Professah with his school," someone shouted.

Hats were passed through the crowd while other men threw bills and small change at Laurence's feet. When it was all gathered together there was more than $50.

A man led up a couple of horses. "You ride one," he said, "and I'll take you back to the chu'ch."

When they drew near the little church, it seemed to be deserted. But as they dismounted and walked toward the door, Laurence heard the mellow voice of prayer—low, humble voices entreating the Lord's mercy.

Laurence and his escort made their way into the church. It was nearly empty, most of the people having fled to their homes. Only a handful of old men remained—a half dozen—who had been down on their knees since Laurence had been taken from them, asking God for the miracle, as He had done once for Daniel when he was thrown in the lion's den, and for the Hebrew children who had been flung into the fiery furnace. . . .

Though they had been praying for his release, when the men heard a noise at the door and, looking up, saw Laurence's figure etched in the afternoon light, they drew back on their knees, their hands clenched in an agony of terror.

"He ain't no ghost!" The white man pushed his way past Laurence into the church toward them. "This is the same man we took away. I mean to come out and hear him myself. He's done us more good today than he's done you-all since he's been here. Next time you plan a meeting, I'll come tell you-all about it." He clapped Laurence's arm in farewell and strode out of the church. The old men, their eyes widened with a joy they had not dared hope for, rushed to Laurence, hugged him, cried over him, sang—and prayed.

At last the little group came out of the church, to find the west aglow with a magnificent sunset, a sunset which Laurence could understandably declare was "the most wonderful I have ever seen."

Word raced joyously from ear to ear, from cabin to cabin, and after supper parents, children, neighbors flocked around the "little 'Fesser" while he told his story.

When at last he went to bed, Laurence fell into an exhausted sleep, only to waken shortly, drenched with the sweat of terror, as he saw red flames licking up from the pile of brush around his feet. . . .

Then, when he was fully awake, to find himself safe in the still peace of a country night, he lay back quietly, thinking of the years behind, the struggle at Piney Woods, the "inchin' along" day by day which must be done.

Once more he saw that sea of faces before him. He thought with what sick horror he had looked into those faces and seen no justice and no compassion to which he might appeal. And yet—they had been there. They had been in the man who for no apparent reason asked for a moment's reprieve and "a speech." They had been in the others who, despite the mob hysteria of which they were a part, could still be reached by honest words. . . . So long as such a thing was possible, the world would never be entirely lost. . . .

Lying back in the soothing country stillness, Laurence felt a sense of peace steal over his exhausted body and mind, and a lift of real hope—hope not only for the colored people for whom he labored, but for the southern white people with whom they lived.

Chapter 16

A Cramped Chance

When the United States entered World War I and all hope of the peace in which he believed was temporarily abandoned, Jones felt there was no choice but to throw his support behind his country, and he made plans to enter officers' training camp at Des Moines, Iowa, where many of his college friends were headed. However, the long arm of necessity reached out to squelch his patriotic decision. His family, in addition to his wife, now consisted of two small sons, his mother-in-law, his mother, whom he had brought down from Marshalltown, Iowa, along with a late-born baby sister Nellie. He had also an unfulfilled contract for eighty lectures on the Chautauqua Circuit, a contract with the Mississippi State Department of Education to serve as director of a summer normal school to train three hundred Negro teachers, and the ever-growing and ever-insistent chores of both keeping the Piney Woods School going and of raising money to finance it.

With a sigh for soldiering, Laurence settled down at his own important job and tried to satisfy his patriotic compulsions "on the side" by serving as the county and state speaker for the Liberty Loans, as chairman of the colored Red Cross for two counties, and as the only colored executive of the First United War Work Drive. Despite its brief existence Piney Woods sent out fifty boys to fight for their country.

Traveling constantly over his section of the state during the next year and a half in his innumerable jobs for the school and the war work, Jones often found himself journeying through the backwoods areas that had seldom seen another visitor. Once, when he was riding horseback through woods on a dim trail, he came out into a clearing where a funeral service was taking place.

133

As he rode into view, one of the group recognized him and hurried to meet him.

" 'Fesser Jones," the man said, " 'Fesser Jones, you'se jes' in time. We ain't got no preacher to bury Brother Bert, and we is so upset about it we don't know what to do. But we couldn't find no one who would come way out hyear. 'Fesser"—the man's eyes gleamed with trust—"you'll read ovah him fo' us, won't you?"

"Of course." Jones climbed off his horse, took his Bible out of his coat pocket, and read a passage from the Scriptures, after which Brother Bert's relatives and friends lowered the body into the woodland grave.

On another trip, Jones was riding close to a dense briar patch when suddenly he became aware of a pair of huge dark eyes staring at him from the inner depths of a thick clump. He reined up his horse and peered into the thicket.

"Who are you?" he asked.

"Mah name's Willie Buck," a frightened adolescent voice floated from the briar patch.

"How old are you?" Jones asked.

"Fo'teen," said the boy.

"Come out and let me look at you," the teacher coaxed. "Have you ever done anything besides farm work?"

The bushes parted and a half-grown barefoot child crawled into view, his head ducked in embarrassment, his torn overalls hanging by one strap.

"Nassuh," Willie said, not meeting Jones's eyes. "Ah ain't done no kind of work 'ceptin' plow and hoe."

"Would you like to come to school and learn something more?"

"Oh, yassuh." Willie's head bobbed up ecstatically, and his bright eyes met the teacher's. "You jes' wait till Ah gets mah shoes." The boy turned and loped off across a field where a cabin could be seen in the distance. Laurence waited until the boy returned, then he pulled him up behind him on the horse, and they headed toward Piney Woods School.

Eight years later Willie Buck graduated from Piney Woods, delivering, for his part in the commencement exercises, a lecture and a demonstration on electricity and the operation of gasoline engines.

The year of 1918 saw the first graduation class at Piney Woods.

There were six members. "How they worked," Principal Jones said of them, "how they loved Piney Woods!"

Three of the girls went on to finish their training as teachers, then came back to serve many years on the Piney Woods faculty.

Charles Shedd, the boy whose father had delivered him to Piney Woods, with a pig for tuition, the day on which Grace Jones arrived as a bride, stayed on at the school to serve as dean of boys and to run the expanding printing department. Of his early years at the school Mr. Shedd remarked, "I came to Piney Woods as a student— handicapped, underprivileged, needing a chance, and willing to pay the price in service whatever way I could. I knocked, and the door was opened unto me."

The graduating class of the following year included Georgia Lee Myers, who had entered Piney Woods by the grace of her amazing list of backers in 1910, and who went out from the school so endowed with the spirit and zeal of Principal and Mrs. Jones that she, single-handed, "scraped up" enough money in the impoverished communities to build, with the help of the Julius Rosenwald Fund, three rural schools before coming back to Piney Woods to take over the elementary department. Of her zealous efforts Jones said, "I only wish I could bring home to people unacquainted with the area what it means to raise six and seven hundred dollars among a people who really want the better things of life but whose ignorance and superstition literally sow with stumbling blocks the path of one who tries to help them."

Principal Jones's eyes were mainly on the underprivileged and ignorant children who without help would have no chance. But such a goal did not exclude an interest in the "especially endowed" who needed a boost to help realize their true potential. A boy by the name of J. R. Oatis came to Piney Woods in the fall of 1918 and entered the eighth grade. Brilliant, imaginative, and ambitious, he had gone as far as he could in his local school, and Piney Woods offered him his only chance for a high-school education. As he says today, "I had ambition and abilities, but what I lacked was direction." Principal Jones quickly sized him up and decided that Piney Woods was not the answer. On his next trip North he arranged for Oatis to attend high school in Three Oaks, Michigan, and take special training in practical farming—his particular interest. There, in addition to going to school, Oatis ran a dairy on the side, and by the time he had finished high school had $1,000 saved up to help toward college expenses. He went to Iowa State College at Ames, later took his doctor's degree at Cornell, where his thesis on farming in the South was so excellent that it became a standard authority on the subject. Today he is president of Alcorn College, the only land-grant agricultural and mechanical college for Negroes in Mississippi.

Principal Jones had good reason to feel that the first decade of Piney Woods more than justified the struggle and the effort that had gone into it. Not only had its graduates carried its spirit out into their own lives and efforts, particularly in the building of schools and helping of other underprivileged children, but the extension work and increased morale which had gone out to the local farmers were paying dividends. In spite of hard times, these farmers had purchased more than six thousand acres of land in the area surrounding Piney Woods—more than had been acquired in the twenty years before the school was established.

As he looked from the cedar-log days to the present bustling little campus with its two hundred students, devoted staff, and on ahead to "a campus on the hill" which, since the war was over, was once more a practical possibility, Principal Jones had every reason to be proud of the progress that had been made. When asked by a curious friend on one of his trips North why he chose to stay in the "backward" South, Jones replied, "I prefer to be a manufacturer of men and women, even under adverse conditions."

It took a northern eye to discover just how adverse those conditions actually were. Doris James, the second white woman to volunteer her services, arrived at Piney Woods in the fall of 1920. A native of Denver, Miss James had decided to join this example of "Christianity in practice" after hearing Principal and Mrs. Jones speak at Des Moines.

She found Professor Jones "a man so absorbed with the future that the present was out of the picture," a man so single-minded about his job and so oblivious to normal physical comforts that he would literally "have not bothered with food or sleep" had not Mrs. Jones and others forced him to.

Immersed as they both were in their common goal of giving a

chance to the endless stream of black children who appeared in the clearing at Piney Woods, neither of the Joneses seemed aware of the privations under which they and their staff lived—the diet of rice and meatless gravy, greens and corn bread, with such delicacies as butter, eggs, coffee, and sweets reserved for "Sunday only"; the prickly straw mattresses on which they all slept; the miserable winter chill of the student-constructed building which made wearing galoshes indoor a necessity to keep the feet from freezing; the only source of heat from front-scorching, back-freezing fireplaces; the only light from kerosene lamps; work hours in which the staff, in imitation of the seemingly tireless pair, labored from 7 A.M. to 9 P.M. in the classrooms, then gave music lessons "after hours" with the result that they frequently became so exhausted that they fell asleep at their desks.

Fired by such a zealous example, Laurence's mother had voluntarily assumed the task of feeding the staff of teachers. Though the cabin in which she and her ten-year-old Nellie lived was so small that she had to feed them in shifts, though her "student help"— terrorized by the old lady's fastidious methods—proved less than adequate, she did what she could with meager supplies to make the teachers' lives more comfortable. Realizing Miss James's and some of the others' dislike for the unleavened meal-and-water corn bread, Gramma Jones made lightbread once a week and also started a few chickens in her yard so that she could occasionally add the luxury of an egg to their diet.

Fragile, still lovely with her dainty features and heavy white hair, Gramma Jones was a lightening influence for the children and teachers alike during that hectic, hard-working winter of 1920. Particularly was she a haven for her own little Nellie and Eula Kelly, a young student whom Grace Jones had taken into her family. " 'Fesser" was a man who not only worked tirelessly himself, but liked to see everyone else, even playful little girls, do the same. But when he would stride in his mother's door, calling ahead, "Where's Eula? Where's Nellie? I've got an errand I want run," Gramma would chase her young imps out the back way, then greet her busy son, murmuring, with an innocent eye, "Why, Lon, I just can't think where those little rascals could have gone to!"

A story of Gramma that became a local legend occurred one day that fall when she decided to take the train to Jackson to do some shopping. An old masher, taking one attentive look at the old lady, bowed low before her and said, "My name is Sam Brown," to which Gramma tartly replied, "Who said it wasn't?"

Working on the theory that "a cramped chance at education is better than none," Laurence and Grace had moved from corner to corner of the campus, giving up their quarters as the space was needed for more students. From their original room in the log cabin they had gone to a corner of the first-built school building, Taylor Hall, and from there to a room and hall in the industrial arts building, and then, when that space was needed, they moved a quarter of a mile off the campus into an old mill house on the railroad. Finally, in 1920, they moved into a small cottage on the edge of the campus which had been built with money donated especially for that purpose by Dr. J. D. Harris. He had been appalled, on a visit in 1919, at the way the couple were living with their two small children.

But such comfort was not for long. The Joneses were sitting at their breakfast on a raw December day, a few days before Christmas, when they were aroused by wild shouts, and looked out of a window to see the boys' dormitory going up in flames.

While the rest of his family and the faculty went out hopelessly to watch the two-story structure crumble to ashes, Laurence sat at his typewriter and began writing letters to friends in the North appealing for funds.

The combination of rough, unseasoned pine lumber, inadequate construction mostly by student labor, and lack of adequate water supply had made fire a constant hazard at Piney Woods. There was no answer in Principal Jones's mind except the building of permanent brick buildings on the hill and the installation of a proper water system.

Yet the feeding and educating of the two hundred students now demanded a minimum of $10,000 each year, and year after year he and Grace faced the summer with no money and no sure promise of any. But this year they would have to do better. Jones was determined, when he saw the boys' dormitory go up in flames that morning, that he had built his last firetrap of pine.

"I don't think letters will do it," Grace told her husband that evening as she looked sadly out at the little campus which now boasted a small "tent city" where the "big boys" were stoically trying to withstand the winter cold in tents borrowed from a nearby lumber camp. The little boys had moved into the teachers' quarters and Miss James and another teacher found their way into the Jones's cottage—making nine people packed into five small rooms. "I think we should go North right now and not wait till spring."

"Perhaps you're right," Laurence answered. "If we were in luck we might send back enough money so they could get the Dulany building up by spring."

Four years before George W. Dulany, a wealthy young Iowan, had sent the first of a series of checks toward the construction of a brick dormitory for girls, to be built and named in honor of "Aunt Lunky," a faithful old colored nurse who had raised the Dulany children, including George. When she died, Aunt Lunky had willed her savings to the Dulany children—savings which amounted to several thousand dollars, and George Dulany planned to send this money in installments to Piney Woods. When Laurence received the first installment he had bought cement and he and his students had dug the foundation for the building up on the hill. The war had stopped the project, but now, since materials were once again available, the time had come when they could go forward.

Principal and Mrs. Jones made hasty plans to go North. When Miss James asked Mrs. Jones about the emotional cost of going off and leaving her two small sons, Grace Jones replied with tears in her bright eyes, "I don't feel that I have the right to let my two stand in the way of the two or three hundred who so need what I can do for them." It was a personal sacrifice that was to shadow both parents' lives.

Spurred by the necessity of their project, the couple put on a whirlwind campaign, speaking several times daily, coaxing, begging, cajoling. Appearing frequently as many as four times a day, between lectures, Mrs. Jones would go from store to store, pleading her cause, picking up a dime, a quarter, a dollar, from whomsoever would listen. Within days the first bank drafts began rolling in at Piney Woods; and Yancy and his crew of students headed up to the abandoned "foundation" on the hill to begin building.

The new project consumed the time of every person connected

with the school. The girls worked sometimes all night on *The Pine Torch,* as they made the endless additions and corrections which the couple sent back by mail and prepared and mailed out the 10,000 copies which went out each month. At the building itself the boys worked long hours with their teachers. It was a hectic season, in which all gave the last measure of their strength toward the common goal. But by commencement week Dulany Hall had been completed —the first building of the future campus—and the girl students made excited plans to move in, leaving their old dormitory for the boys. The Joneses sent word that they would be there for commence- ment, after which they would take a brief rest, then head out again for their summer's soliciting.

And back home, after a winter filled with work, privations, and crises, Miss James still found it in her heart to say of her first hectic year at Piney Woods, "To have known, and worked with, such people, is to have tasted life's honey."

Chapter 17

The Cotton Blossoms

Commencement, that spring of 1921, was a truly memorable one for Piney Woods. Services were held in the new building with Uncle Asa Turner, now chairman of the board of trustees, on hand to help celebrate. But also just as truly it was a "commencement" for the Joneses. Much money must be raised so that the school could move to its permanent home. Grace thought she had an answer.

Song was a natural part of Piney Woods, one which Grace felt might effectively be presented to audiences over the country. Recruiting groups of young singers from the student body would be no problem, since nearly every student who came there could sing— simply, effortlessly, and with remarkable beauty.

Once, when a white visitor was querying Principal Jones about the percentage of students who came, untrained, into Piney Woods, and who could sing naturally without instruction, Laurence made, what seemed on the surface, a wild generality, "Any four colored boys are a quartet."

His visitor was amazed at such a seemingly absurd statement from a usually cautious, level-headed man.

"Any four?" he questioned, with raised eyebrows.

"Any four," Laurence insisted. "Look out there now." He pointed to where groups of boys were on their way to class. "Pick any of the boys at random and we will see."

His guest pointed out four boys each from a different group and they were called over. Jones explained to these boys that they were to sing as a quartette. "I'll give you five minutes," he said. "Now you go in a huddle and choose your song—any one you wish—and come back here and sing it for us."

The boys grinned their willingness, walked out of earshot, and conferred, then one of them came back. "We fo' ain't nevah sung together, 'Fesser," he said.

141

"That is good," the principal said. "Go select your song and your parts."

As Jones and his guest watched them, they put their heads together as if doing a bit of preliminary harmonizing, then came back, and at a signal from one of them they broke into "Joshua Fit de Battle of Jericho"—one boy sailing into the tenor part, another sliding down into the bass, while the other two took the between parts, then all four closed in a tight, skin-tingling harmonious finale.

"Thank you," Jones said. "Now all of you hurry on to your classes."

"You win," Jones's guest said, shaking his head, "but I never would have believed it."

"It was a broad statement," Laurence admitted, "and I wouldn't have made it anywhere else in the country. But here in Piney Woods I've never seen it fail—these children were *born* with music in their souls."

Grace's idea was to utilize this innate musical ability to help raise money.

"I think I'll take a group of student singers out with me this summer," she said to her husband. "It will be a wonderful experience for them to get out and see the country and meet people in different places, and if it proves out, we might keep groups of them out all year round."

"If we could," Laurence agreed, "it would keep them away from here when we're so short of space, as well as keep up the soliciting. I've wondered about taking students along with us—they're certainly good witnesses of the work we're doing down here. But there's just one thing wrong."

"What's that?"

"You know what traveling's like—just for us. It will be much more difficult with a group of students. Perhaps if we had special equipment of some kind—such as house cars with facilities for cooking and sleeping—then it might work out."

"First let's try it out," Grace said. "I'll take a group of boys out this summer and then when we get money ahead we will buy the right kind of equipment."

"The most we could start with this year is that secondhand car the dealer at Jackson is trying to sell the school," Laurence said.

"But we don't have money for hotel rooms, even if you could get them, and that car wouldn't do to eat and sleep in."

"Let's get the car and try it for a season, since we need some kind of automobile here anyhow," Grace suggested. "I'll take a quartette and you go on with your lecture tour and we will see how it works out. As for food and sleep, we'll manage."

"I'm certain you will," agreed her husband soberly, "but I hate to see you take on a job like that."

"I was born for 'a job like that,'" smiled Mrs. Jones.

The seven-passenger open touring car was purchased and with her quartette, "The Cotton Blossoms," keyed up to sing spirituals like they had never been sung before, Grace headed North.

She was not long in finding out that she had taken on a difficult assignment. It had been one thing to travel as a lone woman, or with her husband, but it was something else again to get accommodations for her quartette of big back-country boys, her own two little sons, and twelve-year-old Eula Kelly who had come along with "Mama" to look after the little boys.

Eula was a new addition to the Jones family. Three years before this slender, bright-eyed, intelligent child had come to Piney Woods from a neighboring town. Because of her quick mind and lively good humor, plus the fact that she was too young for a boarding student, the Joneses had moved her in with them, and when her own family had moved North, Eula, given the choice, had elected to stay with "Mama and Papa" Jones, and had become a part of the intimate family group—an energetic and devoted part for which busy Grace Jones was infinitely thankful.

Now, while she left her little band to sit in a park and rest and play, with reliable Eula in charge of little Turner and Laurence, Junior, Grace could drive ahead into the next town and arrange bookings for the day—chances to sing in churches, before civic clubs, for private parties, or in hotels, the bookings ranging from one to six performances a day depending on how many she could set up.

After a few performances Grace learned that it was better to appear without charge, and then after they had mellowed the audience with their stirring music, to tell about Piney Woods and ask for donations. If the members of the audience had paid even a nominal sum then that made it easy to keep from donating. Few people, she discovered, like to reach into their pockets the second time.

To feed her brood, Mrs. Jones relied mainly on cold things that they could buy and take out—to eat picnic style—by the roadside or in public parks. When they had time they bought food which could be cooked over an open fire. But hot foods came mostly when some group offered to feed them after a performance. A great number of church groups, in appreciation of the concert, provided a hot supper for the performers. This became a play game with them—to "wish" on the good graces of a group that they might be fed.

The baggage of the traveling troupe was strapped to the big old touring car. The suits in which the boys sang somehow must be kept clean, and the tents to sleep in must be guarded. Even if they had had the money to pay for hotel accommodations, which they did not, Grace knew from her own experience that in most cases rooms would be denied them. It was lucky for her, though, that this first tour was through Iowa where she knew a lot of people, for when the weather was bad, which fortunately it was not most of the time, it would not do for the singers and the young children to sleep in the wet and cold.

When bad weather caught them, she made the rounds, pleading for the basement of a church, a railroad station, or any dry place of shelter, and when that failed, as it did a time or two, they simply "stacked up" in the car with the storm curtains up. A few times they were given hotel accommodations, but not often. One night a compassionate hotel manager let them spend the night in his office.

But despite the privations the summer was a success. By the personal contacts of the singing groups—visual evidence of what the school was doing coupled with the emotional appeal of the music—Grace was able to raise far more money than she had the summer before. In addition, many names of people who had shown a vital interest in the program were added to the list that received *The Pine Torch.*

Laurence, too, had had a successful summer. It had started off in surprising good humor when he had accompanied Uncle Asa Turner back to Iowa. When Captain Turner had first suggested they make the trip together, Laurence had not known what to do. It had always galled him to have to ride in the Jim Crow car till the train got out of the South, even when he paid first-class fare, but to have his friend witness this kind of indignity hurt even worse.

But he had not reckoned on Uncle Asa's sensitivity and understanding. Before boarding the train the shrewd old man told him his plans.

"I've got it all figured out, Laurence," he said. "I know you don't want to make any trouble and I don't intend to ride most to Iowa without having the opportunity of talking with you, so we will fool them."

"How?"

Captain Turner straightened up to every inch of his impressive height, his noble old head with its flowing white hair set off by sparkling eyes. "Don't I strike you, young man, as an old rascal important enough and rich enough to carry my own valet with me?"

Laurence's shoulders shook with laughter as he caught on. "A difference in size helps, too," he admitted. "Besides, I look small enough beside you to be your shine boy."

"And young enough, too." Uncle Asa smiled. "How you keep that undergraduate look and do the work you do I'll never know."

"Perhaps that is the answer," Laurence said. "I haven't time to grow old."

At traintime in Jackson a rangy, impressive-looking old man handed his little black bag to the small colored man beside him, then strode onto the train, his "boy" following. They were comfortably ensconced in the "white" Pullman section, and when the conductor came through to collect tickets, Captain Turner handed him both of theirs, saying carelessly, as the official examined them, "George, take off my shoes and fetch my slippers, my feet are hurting me."

"Yassuh," murmured the dark man at his side, "right away, Cap'n." Laurence opened Uncle Asa's bag and took out a pair of house slippers.

The conductor returned to Uncle Asa his part of the tickets and passed on without a murmur. As the door closed behind him, since there were no other people close to them, they broke into delighted chuckles.

"Worked, didn't it, son?" grinned the old man with a happy

wink. "I've always heard that nurses, valets, and maids were allowed to ride with their employers even if they are colored. I've never had a valet, but I thought it was worth trying."

A few minutes later, as the two friends were busily talking about Piney Woods, Uncle Asa glanced up to see another conductor bearing down upon them.

"George," he ordered, breaking off his conversation, "get me my medicine, I'm feeling faint."

Obediently "George" reached into the little bag and got out a bottle of medicine. When the official was out of earshot the two men picked up the thread of their conversation.

Between the two of them the Joneses raised enough money to operate the school for another year and build a second permanent building up on the hill. When finished, Goodwill Hall, the main school building, took its proper place on that horseshoe drive. Laurence had long ago hired a professional landscaper and architect to design the campus, so that though sporadically built, it would never be haphazard.

It looked now as though the haunts of the Dog-eater would know him no more.

Chapter 18

"Lay My Burdens Down"

"The Cotton Blossoms," groups of both boy and girl singers, proved, as Mrs. Jones had predicted, the key to the problem of keeping a steady flow of money and other gifts coming in to Piney Woods. Year after year they toured the country, from one end to the other, in a constant stream. New buildings sprang up on that "magic" horseshoe circle up on the hill until, finally, most of the school's activities were conducted there. All of the available farm land was in cultivation and more land was bought. Yet still a larger and larger stream of children came wanting the gift of education.

With the aid of a Community House, a substantial but simple two-story brick building where they lived, the Joneses were able to entertain their visitors from the North who wanted to see how the money they contributed was spent. Their coming helped in other ways. More and more the brighter boys and girls at the school were sent on with help from friends of the school to where they could get educational facilities more in keeping with their talents.

Though the bulk of the students offered some possibilities of grading—unlike the seventeen-year-old first graders and the sixty-year-old auditors when the school first started—Piney Woods still boasted an extraordinary range. There was one sixth grader who claimed that he was "somewhere around forty" although he did not know the exact age. There were a number of children under the twelve-year minimum set for boarding students who were simply left at the school by parents too poor or too troubled to care for them.

One small boy was found wandering alone along the campus walk, with no belongings save a new pencil clutched in his tiny fist, who refused to talk with anyone except " 'Fesser Jones." When he was taken to the principal he explained that he was an orphan without any place to live and that he had heard that " 'Fesser Jones" took little boys in if they wanted to learn, and he had a pencil which he considered the key to beginning this process. Nobody knew what his name was, so he was taken in, given a name, and started to school.

Then there was "Pa" Collins—a man so imbued with the desire for education that, although he had neither the money nor the time for school, solved the problem by simply moving in with, as someone said, "a passel of kids" and a wife. All of the Collinses worked for the school, in exchange for the privilege of living in a cabin on the school grounds, and with "Pa," all of them, as the children became old enough, except Mrs. Collins, attended classes. By the time "Pa" had worked his way up to the eighth grade he had eight children. When he was in the tenth grade the number of children had increased to ten, and when he finally graduated from the twelfth grade there were twelve of them. As he stood proudly in the line of graduates, between two of his sons, someone in the audience shouted, "For God's sake, 'Fesser Jones, don't you promote that man no more."

Then there were subnormal "problem" children and cripples. The Joneses could no more turn these down than the others.

It was not too much to say that for the majority of the children who came to Piney Woods that theirs was not bridging the gap from kerosene lamps to electricity but from pine torches to electricity. Certainly few who waited for and read *The Pine Torch* avidly every month, or who heard "The Cotton Blossoms" sing, or even those who visited the school and saw with their own eyes, actually realized the tremendous jump most of the students had taken.

One particularly bright girl was sent into the home of a wealthy Iowa woman where she was to help around the house in exchange for room and board so that she could attend college.

"Go down into the cellar and bring up the dustpan," the woman told her the first day she was to help with the housecleaning.

She stared wide-eyed with dismay. It came as a distinct shock to the woman, when she finally caught on, that the girl had never heard of a dustpan or knew what a cellar was.

This was not unusual at Piney Woods. The students who came

there, now that the new plant up on the hill had some modern conveniences, had to be taught how to turn on or turn off a water faucet, and many of the children for months after they came considered an electric light or a telephone an instrument of "the devil."

For the indefatigable principal and his equally indefatigable wife there was no letup. Every year the expense of running the school increased. Every corner had to be cut. The custom of bartering the various items that were sent to the school became even more a part of civic help to the community. Now officially called "Lunky Day," in honor of Aunt Lunky, the first Saturday of every month reemphasized the need for more and more help. People—both white and black—came for miles to get "clo's fo' de chilluns" or "somethin' black fo' a funeral," or articles of clothing or furniture to piece out following a fire. Women with babies in their arms and "eight or ten mo' " back home offered a "sack of peas" or reached down into their bosoms or stocking tops for a bit of rag in which they had tied their precious cash to buy something desperately needed. In the winter months boys tagged along wearing run-over and worn-down high-heeled women's shoes which their mothers hoped to replace with something more substantial. Holiday season— Christmastime—was the most heartbreaking of all when mothers begged for "a piece of ribbon or a doll" for "mah chilluns" who otherwise would have no Christmas at all.

Those who had nothing to exchange either in produce or cash were given the things they needed the most if the school had them.

The crushing need of both the community and the school was so great that any personal desire that either Laurence or Grace had for a little rest or a slackening of their labors faded in the face of scenes like these.

When they were not out on their endless tours, speaking, booking their singers, making contacts, Grace Jones threw any residue of energy that she had left into agitating for prison reforms on the home front, and it was through her efforts that a state reform school was eventually instituted so that the colored youngsters were no longer thrown in jails and prisons with hardened criminals. In addition she worked for and reorganized the Colored Federation of Women's Clubs for the state.

Laurence was on the road constantly, often driving all night long after making a speech, so that he would be in the next town where he was scheduled to appear. It was nothing for him to go ten and twelve hours, during the day, without food.

Their chief reward for this strenuous work came during the hours they were back on the campus when they could take short walks to visit the various shops, inspect the kitchens, the sewing rooms, the gardens and the fields, from which rose the joyous songs of boys and girls who were going to have a chance for a better life.

It was particularly gratifying on opening or commencement days to hear the same boys and girls who had come to the school as almost tongue-tied youngsters speak out freely and without embarrassment about what they were doing, and with eager eyes tell about what they planned to do.

There was one boy who said that he was going to take his father's wornout farm and build it up while his father went into town and got a job. There was a girl who proudly told how she made enough out of a summer's work to "pay ahead" for a full year's schooling. She had cut brush, planted corn, dug potatoes, picked and canned blackberries, set type, washed and ironed, milked a couple of cows each morning. Then, to further help out, when she went home for a week, she helped with cotton picking, stripped sugarcane, and taught her mother how to can blackberries.

Then there were the relaxing laughs only barely removed from heartaches in letters sent to the school. "Now father were expecting to help me by selling a cow but the cow eat so many acorns she died so father say he can let you have some molasses if they will be all rite for pay. If they dont do then i will hafter come and be a work boy as we aint got no money and i sure does want to edicate. Rite me al about it cause i will work at *anything,* and the boy that are coming with me are going to let you have a young heifer for his scholing. yours truly, Doc Bryant."

For such students school meant life; arithmetic a means to determine the cost of seed; chemistry a technique for making molasses, testing seed corn or curing ham; blacksmithing and shoe-mending a way to get a "salaried" job—or perhaps owning a small shop. From where they had come it was a tremendous step, the opening door of life which held a promise other than "sowbelly and srhdown."

But as each year passed, the funds needed for running the school, in addition to building and expanding, mounted. In 1925 it had risen to $30,000, and each year increased. Every cent of the increase had to be, as it were, "freshly won" each season.

Making three and four tours each year both of the Joneses reached out for every gift from pennies to thousands. They made no distinction to whom they appealed—the call was to the heart, and any size contribution was received with gratitude. On their list of donors were men of great fortunes such as Mentholatum's A. A. Hyde, chewing gum's Colonel William Wrigley, Major Max Fleischman, George Foster Peabody, and hotel porters, farmers' wives, and bootblacks. One old colored man, with no family of his own, went to the county farm to spend his last days and gave his all, more than $5,000, to the school.

In 1927 the problem of taking "The Cotton Blossoms" out was made much easier when A. A. Hyde presented a house car to the school. A big, well-finished affair, it boasted of bunk beds that pulled down like Pullman berths, cooking facilities, and even a rug on the floor. So charmed was Mrs. Jones with such luxurious equipment that she headed out on a tour that ranged from California to New England and which lasted eighteen months and raised thousands of dollars.

When she finally got back to Piney Woods, she looked ill, and under her husband's insistent questioning admitted that she felt exhausted. He put her to bed and called the doctor at Jackson. The diagnosis was pneumonia.

Word quickly spread over the campus, and the community and a steady stream of visitors and well-wishers streamed to the Community House. They all came, white and colored, wanting to help this woman who had been so good to them. Grace rallied, and the verdict of the three doctors on the case lifted the hearts of her husband, students, and friends who had kept an hourly vigil. "She will get well," the doctors said.

She did—to the point of sitting up and doing a little desk work in her room and receiving the daily flood of well-wishers who arrived with their flowers, cakes, and tempting foods.

One day a white friend of Grace's came and the two women had a spirited discussion about a certain type of needlework in which

Grace was interested as an addition to the work done in one of her handcraft classes. Carried away with her ideas, she left her room and went down to the office in the school to find some patterns to show to her visitor.

It was a raw, chilly day and there had been no fire in the little office for many weeks. Grace, in her restless, energetic fashion, kept looking through patterns for the one that she wanted.

Her husband, coming home and finding her gone, rushed down to the office, and, with a sickening wave of fear, found her standing in the cold, damp room busily pawing through her files. He led her back to the warm house.

"Why didn't you have someone light a fire for you?" he asked.

"Oh," Grace laughed, "I was in a hurry. Besides, I feel fine."

That night, almost without warning, she slipped into a coma. Doctors were hurriedly summoned, but although they worked with her until the next day she never regained consciousness.

It was a shattering blow. Not only the terrible loss to her husband and young sons, her devoted friends and helpers, but to the school. It was months before they all could realize just how many jobs this amazing woman had filled: teacher, director of two departments, solicitor, office manager, hostess, and a friend to everyone. That one person had carried them all—and with such vitality, graciousness, and charm—was almost unbelievable. It literally took half a dozen to absorb the jobs she had carried alone.

The shock to her husband was staggering. In one sweep he had lost wife, confidant, friend and the greatest "partner" he would ever know. He had also lost the mother of his young sons—boys who, to their parents' mutual regret, had so often been "shuffled around" in the interest of the endless horde of children whose welfare so consumed the minds and hearts of their parents. And now Laurence had them alone—the eleven- and fourteen-year-old adolescents he had scarcely had time to know. He realized that now, more than ever, they were doomed, like "Topsy," to just grow, now that with Grace gone his work alone out in the field meant the sole difference between the loss or survival of the school that she had come to love so devoutly.

They buried her down under the old cedar tree where, as a bride, she had taken up the burden of this mutual dream.

Chapter 19

Taking the Ditch

In the decade following his wife's death in 1928, Jones tore into his work with a dogged dedication that was almost frightening to those close to him. But the job of singlehandedly financing an ever-expanding school through the depression years was a burden that did not permit letting up for a moment. In order to spend more and more time soliciting he learned increasingly to delegate his duties at the school.

In a way it was good for him to travel. In addition to the void left so painfully evident at the school by the death of Mrs. Jones, most of the old familiar faces were gone also. John Webster, the mainstay of Jones's early years, had sold out his Mississippi holdings and left the state. Uncle Asa Turner was dead, as was Uncle Ed Taylor and sweet, lovable Amon Gibson. Bandy-legged Uncle Tom had laid his musket down for good. However, in their places, as was to happen so often in the future, had emerged another flock of faithfuls. Mrs. Singleton, a colored friend from Iowa, had come down to run the Community House and to look after Laurence's two boys; Eula Kelly had finished a business course in Iowa and was now supervising "The Cotton Blossoms." Singleton Bender, a farm boy from Jones County who had entered Piney Woods as a ninth-grade student in 1926, had proved so reliable an addition to the school that he had already graduated from Cotton Blossom singer to quartette manager, and was now taking groups out alone over the country. Mr. Floyd Herrington, who had taken over Webster's holdings, was as stanch a friend of the school as Webster, particularly of its music department, and helped both with funds and equipment during crises. Wilk Kelly, the curious towhead of Jones's first visit to Webster, had moved to the campus with his wife and children to take over Uncle Tom's post as guard, only now it was a full-fledged job of "night watchman" with a little tower to sit in and a big electric lantern to patrol with.

Though cash was hard come by, fortunately enough the school "ate better" during the depression than it had during the years before. The gardens, orchards, and fields were now in full-scale production, yielding over half of the total food consumption. A small herd of Ayrshires, donated to the school by A. A. Hyde in 1920, had increased to the point where the milk and butter needs were adequately supplied, and an occasional butchering furnished fresh meat.

Despite the main buildings of brick, fire still proved the greatest hazard at Piney Woods. After a cottage burned in which several young boys nearly lost their lives, Jones was able to stir up enough interest in Jackson and the nearby communities for the purchase and installation of a water system adequate for a community of two thousand.

As the graying hairs of middle age came, with the slightly stockier body and the grim determination which took away the boyishness of his face, coupled with an honorary degree or so, the "little 'Fesser" more and more was addressed as "Dr. Jones" or "President Jones." But to the wide-eyed children of the piney woods this man who spent his strength "scrapping up" the money to provide them with an education and with hope, and who, no matter how exhausted, always had time to respond to the pressure of a small hand, or a questioning voice, remained "Papa" or "Daddy."

To keep up the interest in the school, Jones relied heavily on "The Cotton Blossoms," sending out as many as a dozen troupes at once in house cars, under Eula's supervision. At home a baseball diamond was laid out that was not only the envy of the local white community, who used it for their matched games, but which developed such fine teams that Jones also began sending his baseball nines out to compete with other clubs and thereby arouse more interest in the school.

In spite of these activities, however, he never failed to keep the primary purpose of his school at the center of his activities and his interest. No matter where he went, those back at the school never knew what he would turn up with when he arrived home. Mrs.

Singleton, and, later, Eula, who replaced her as hostess of the Community House, learned to plan for and to expect anything.

Once, when he was driving back from Hattiesburg, Jones's ever-searching eyes fell on a shy-eyed, ragged girl walking along the highway clutching books to her thin chest. He slowed down his car and called to her. The frightened girl took one look at the strange man in the car and, like a terrified rabbit, scuttled for home. Jones turned into a side lane where she had fled and saw her disappear in a one-room shack. He drove up to it, got out, went to the door, and knocked. The door finally opened an inch or so and her frightened eyes peered out.

"Is your mama home?" he asked.

Some of the fear faded from the child's face at the gentleness of his voice. "Nossuh," she said, "she won't be home for a nuthah half houah."

"Then I'll wait out here," said Jones, as he sat down and leaned against the wall of the cabin.

The child studied him through the crack, then slowly opened the door and sidled out. She stood on one foot and then the other, as if keeping herself in readiness to run on a moment's notice.

"Where do you go to school?" he asked.

"Pine Ridge, suh."

"Do you like to go to school?"

"Oh, yassuh." The girl's thin face lighted briefly, then became sad. "Only dis is mah las' year."

"Would you like to go to high school?"

"High school!" The child's eyes grew large. "Dey ain't no high school roun' hyear."

"Would you work if you could go?"

"Work!" The girl's shyness completely left her in the heat of her intensity. She rushed over and clutched his sleeve. "Mistah, if you could make it so's I could go on to school, Ah'd chop cotton or strip cane or plow or hoe. Why, I'd even *get down on my knees* and scrub floors!"

"*Down on my knees!*" In a way this was the girl's supreme offer, for this was one of the chief taboos that Laurence and his teachers had had to fight. Ever since their freedom from slavery the southern Negroes had thought of being on their knees as a symbol of their former status, and the right to stand on your own feet and not "knee down" to anyone save the Lord was a precious symbol of their new freedom. Time after time girls had come to Piney Woods who, given the task of mopping a room, would stand in the center and throw a bucket of water across the floor, then follow it with a broom rather than get down and scrub, as they had been told to do. Actually one of the teachers, who had a girl assigned to keep her house scrubbed, one day dropped a spoon back of the cookstove and when she stooped over to get it, saw a big hole cut in the floor under the stove. When she asked the girl how this had happened, the child explained, without embarrassment, that she had cut it so that the water, as she mopped, would go through it, rather than for her to have to get down on her knees to finish her job.

That this girl would volunteer to work on her knees impressed Jones.

"You may have to do just that," he told her, "for I am going to give you a chance."

When he drove up to the Community House later in the day he had the girl with all her belongings ready to enroll.

On a trip North, late in 1929, as he walked along the streets of a large city, his sympathetic eye caught sight of a little blind black girl standing on a street corner holding out a tin cup for passersby to drop coins into. Though barely on time for his speaking engagement, Jones stopped and chatted with the small ragged urchin and found out her name and where she lived. The next day, when he caught the train to Piney Woods, she was on the seat beside him.

This seemed too much to his devoted, overworked staff. There was no doubt about the need of this child, but there was equally no doubt that the school was not equipped to take care of her special case. No one knew Braille, no one was trained to work with blind children.

"We'll see," said Principal Jones, with instructions to one of the teachers to clean up the little girl, make her comfortable, and as nearly as possible make her feel at home. Then he began investigating.

He made the shocking discovery that although Mississippi had a school for crippled colored children, there were no facilities whatsoever for the colored blind. Senator Jesse Adams, himself blind, and

Mrs. S. A. McBryde were, through a state commission, trying to stir up the necessary interest to provide such a school, but the appropriation that had been made was not sufficient to build one. Working with Senator Adams and Mrs. McBryde, Jones succeeded in locating the colored blind school at Piney Woods. The appropriation amounted to enough to pay a meager salary to one trained teacher and supply board and lodging for ten students. The building was Piney Woods' problem.

Jones hired a teacher, Mis Martha Morrow, from the Overbrook School for the Blind in Philadelphia, and had a small cottage built on the campus to house Miss Morrow and her ten charges.

It was not long until she had made heart-warming progress! Of those original ten—children who had never before had any of the special training that their handicap required—there was one girl of fourteen who had never been in any sort of school in her life, or worn shoes, or heard of a church. There was a boy of seventeen who was delivered to Piney Woods just at the point where he had been slated to be sent to the poor farm along with his grandfather. There was a child of seven who was so frightened and nervous that it took weeks of patient coaxing before he could bring himself to speak out loud.

In the twenty years that Piney Woods had helped "forgotten" children, none had been quite so pathetically forgotten as these.

Then, three years later, just as the results of sympathetic teaching were beginning to pay off in terms of a normal life filled with singing, reading, writing, and handicrafts for these sightless unfortunates, the state cut off any further appropriation for the colored blind.

Soul sick, Miss Morrow went to see Dr. Jones. To her amazement, instead of the dejection she anticipated, the "little 'Fesser" did not appear downhearted.

"I've been thinking this through," Jones said, "and I think I've figured out an answer."

"But they've cut us off," said Miss Morrow. "There will be no money for my salary, for our board and room, for the Braille books and slates. You can't afford to absorb an additional load like that!"

"Nor can we disband your school," Jones said flatly. "Why, look what you've been able to do already! I've never seen such rapid

changes as have occurred in those children. It would be criminal to
stop now."

"It would be," the teacher agreed, "but you can't sacrifice all of
Piney Woods to my little group!"

"I don't intend to," Principal Jones said decisively. "Piney
Woods is a work school where students have a chance to pay their
way. Why can't we give the blind children that same opportunity?"

"But how? They can't work in the gardens or in the kitchens or
in the dairy. Of course they can make brooms and sew a little, but
not enough to pay the expenses."

"They can sing," Jones cried out triumphantly. "You know how
often you've remarked about the special talents your students have
for music. We will organize a quartette and send it out in one of
the house cars, on a tour, so they can sing before groups and tell
their story. Surely that would be appealing enough to raise the
money they need."

Although it did not pay all of the expenses, it paid enough so
that the school could absorb the rest. And it spread the story of
Piney Woods that had taken care of the colored blind in Mississippi
when the state itself would do nothing for them. For another ten
years both the work and the expenses were taken care of, with
Jones and his staff working just a little harder, and during that
time for three years a blind student was valedictorian of the graduating class.

It was not until 1945, when Helen Keller visited Piney Woods and
went on from there, to appear before the state legislature where she
appealed for adequate state aid for the colored blind, that an appropriation was set up which provided sufficient funds to build a
small school for them in Jackson. When that school was completed
in 1950, Miss Morrow became its principal and moved into her new
quarters with her students. Piney Woods, however, had not seen
the last of its blind students. Many came back, after finishing their
elementary training, to take advantage of its high school and junior
college departments.

By the end of the 1930's Piney Woods had, in addition to its
blind department, five hundred regular students. That took a lot of
food, a lot of clothes, a lot of books, and much money for the staff,
even if they worked for almost nothing. Through the sincerity of his

appeal, Jones had already made, and continued to make, many devoted friends for the school, men and women who recognized an "honest job for humanity" and who unbuttoned their purses along with their hearts. But to reach and keep in contact with all of these donors meant unremitting toil, everlasting patience, and a contagious zeal which transmitted itself to his helpers. Fortunately Jones's amazing vitality withstood the driving pace. Weary nights after weary nights he fell into bed too tired even to read. It was then that he amused himself, those few exhausted moments before sleep, with memories out of his childhood, memories of pleasures he had known in the days when he had had time to know them; snatches of poetry, favorite books. He thought one night with wry amusement that he had as a boy read *Robinson Crusoe* at least once each month for several years and now he was lucky to find time for a glance at the evening newspaper. But it was good to recall moments of pleasure, of laughter, of lavish childish dreams so different from the task that he had assumed.

Eula Kelly and Georgia Myers and most of the oldtimers who had known him for years worried about "Papa" Jones and the terrific pace he was maintaining. But somehow he managed to last. And, after all, as he reminded them, there was so much to do, and no one else to do it.

Driving home late one night, after a speaking engagement in Laurel, Mississippi, as Jones rounded a curve he saw in front of him a wrecked car endways across the road, and beside it a woman and several children who, if he kept on, he could not avoid hitting. In a split second he realized also that he could not stop his own car. Without a moment's hesitation he swerved his car to one side over a ten-foot embankment. There was a crunching noise and then silence. After a few moments in clearing his jarred head Jones realized that he was still alive and apparently unhurt. He hurriedly crawled out of his wrecked car, scrambled up the embankment, and helped move the wrecked car to one side to prevent another accident like his.

A Jackson newspaper, describing the incident, switched from straight news reporting to editorializing, with the comment that "all of us who are acquainted with Professor Jones realize that he has spent a lifetime taking the ditch in the interests of other people."

But that is what he had chosen to do, and after a quarter of a century in doing it he wrote in 1935: "If I had my life to live over again I would do exactly as I have done and start Piney Woods School. But," he added poignantly, "I would try to live more fully as I went along. Most of all, I would be kinder. I would not be less charitable but I would be more of a friend.

"The busy man is to be pitied, for he pays such a price for his busy hours. The flower of life nourishes on leisure, and of that he takes little. Family life, friendships, and ordinary humanity suffer. I feel that I have cheated myself in these things; brick and stone and their effect on other lives can never make up to me what the confidence and intimacy of my sons would have given. I wanted to help a thousand lads. . . ."

Chapter 20

White Folks' Religion

"White folks' religion," which has always been puzzling to the Negro who takes the teachings of Christ as literal instructions for daily life, provided its share of problems on "The Cotton Blossoms" tours. Dr. Jones was adamant that all of the Piney Woods contact with the public should be, as his own had been, without incident that might lead to hard words and trouble. And yet it was most difficult for Eula Kelly and Miss James, who helped her with the tours, or any of the staff that accompanied the young singers, to explain satisfactorily to them how people could follow a faith that claims that all men are brothers and then consider their colored brothers unworthy to enter their churches, as worshipers, or even sleep in their basements after giving a concert in the church.

A colored person, particularly colored persons raised in the simple literalism of the rural southern churches, believes that his religion means something because it has made him do as Christ said, turn the other cheek when hit by the white man on one. It has helped him "take low" in every difference with the white man, and has given him the grace not to hate the man who made him do so. But it is most difficult for him to see that the white man's religion bears any such fruit.

But "Papa" Jones, who depended upon "The Cotton Blossoms" tours not only to help finance the school but looked upon them as a living example of interracial good will, gave implicit instructions to Eula: "Don't jump on things like a dog on a bone. You'll run into a lot of things you won't like, but keep your head and don't allow yourself ever to become angry. Just remember, that you're responsible not just to Piney Woods and to me but to the whole human race."

It was quite an order, one that at times demanded almost super-

161

human restraint. But Eula Kelly had had good training. Traveling first with "Mama" Jones, in the old touring car, she had had a chance to study her adopted mother's winning ways, the combination of persistence and diplomacy with which she had gone about getting bookings, arranging to appear before special organizations, providing shelter for the singers, and in making her pleas for donations.

When Eula was only sixteen years old, they had a quartette of "The Cotton Blossoms" touring through New England when Mrs. Jones received an emergency call from her husband to join him in Boston. "Here, Eula," Mrs. Jones had said, "you manage the singers for the rest of the season. You have watched me long enough to know how. You'll know what to do."

Eula had never been so frightened in her life. "Know what to do!" Here she was off in a strange part of the country with four young singers, with no money, and no bookings ahead. "But I can't," she gasped.

Grace Jones smiled that wise smile of hers, patted Eula affectionately on the arm, and said, "Oh, yes, you can. Besides, there is no other way. I have to join Laurence. Remember, Eula, we are counting on you."

Mrs. Jones went on to Boston, leaving behind a half-grown frightened child faced with a terrifying responsibility far beyond her age and experience.

"In the rest of that season," Eula Kelly Moman said many years later, "I changed from a child to an adult."

And of course, as Mrs. Jones knew she would, she made it, just as all of them did when Piney Woods needed it. There simply was no other way.

It was fortunate that she had the training because after Mrs. Jones's death the responsibility for this important phase of the school's financing fell on her shoulders.

Southern born and bred, there were many things that she had to learn on these tours. Simply crossing the Mason and Dixon's line by no means meant that the disadvantage of being a colored person ceased to exist. Oftentimes it increased them. There were certain freedoms in the North, it was true, but if anyone had the illusions that the same freedoms existed for a colored person as for a white they were certain to be soon shattered.

In the South the taboos had been, for the most part, definite. For instance, you must go to the back door of a restaurant for food but in most cases you would be able to buy it there. In the North, the taboos were more illusive and frequently more cruel. A restaurant would mysteriously be "full up," although vacant tables were right in front of them, and there was no "back door" to which to go. She found that though she, as a lone woman, might take a table in a café, when she entered the same café with her quartette of boys, she almost certainly would be greeted, "Sorry, but we can't serve you."

And there were other things that she had to learn. Different sections of a state might vary greatly in their prejudices, and you had to learn local customs by experience.

One thing that bothered her and the boys for a long time was that in the New England states the audiences seldom clapped, and at first, after a program with no applause, she hesitated to ask for donations. But then she found that this same group might give them an enthusiastic welcome to come back the next year, as well as a generous contribution. She also learned that people in the rural sections of the East thought of all Negro singers as "minstrels," and would frequently inquire of the spiritual singing "Cotton Blossoms," "When is your minstrel show going to start?"

She also learned that a trip to the far-off New England states might change the range of her adolescent singers and that she ran the risk of "carrying out a tenor and coming back with a baritone!" After a few such experiences she soon learned to carry "a spare tire" in the person of a younger tenor, thereby necessitating taking along an extra person.

The house cars were excellent for summer and spring weather but as Piney Woods grew and more and more groups were sent out, many of them went in the wintertime. And the house cars simply were not built for extremely cold weather.

One night, as Eula's quartette finished a long program, with five or six encores at the demand of an unusually enthusiastic audience, Eula discovered that while the program had been going on a blizzard had blown up. When the crowd had filed out, she asked the minister of the church, where the concert had been held, if she and the boys might sleep in the basement of the church to stay warm. The answer was a red-faced, eye-averted, but positive, "No." Eula held her temper, in compliance with "Papa" Jones, and, as he had suggested, went on in her quietest, most pleasant voice to explain that they were in a house car, that it offered little protection against the weather, and that she had been unable to get a place for them to stay at a hotel. The answer was a more emphatic "No" as the minister turned his back and walked away.

Eula and her quartette fortunately possessed strong constitutions, strong enough to even doze a bit in the frightfully cold inside the car as the blizzard raged outside. There were icicles hanging in their faces from the roof of the car when morning came.

Once, as she prepared a season's schedule, Eula accepted an invitation from a church in New England in which they had sung before, but noted that it had a new minister. When they arrived in the village where this church was, they parked their car beside it, as they had done the year before, to make use of the facilities in the basement. But when Eula went to get the key the new minister did not "know where it was." She explained about the former visit, and that the previous minister had them park their car there, gave them the key to the basement, and let them use the plumbing facilities. The minister hedged, but when she persisted he finally "found" the key for her. As she left, she heard him say to an assistant, "I don't like to do that! You just never know what a nigger will do."

Eula felt the hot blood rise in her cheeks, counted ten, thought of "Papa's" stern, "Now don't you jump on things!" but she was still trembling when she reached the car. She said nothing to the boys about what she had overheard, unlocked the door, and they used the facilities in the basement and went on with the concert. But next morning, as they were ready to leave, Eula cornered the minister and told him that she had overheard his remark.

"Now I don't know whether you realize it or not," she continued, "but to me the term 'nigger' means an unreliable person. I consider both myself and my boys as completely reliable. We have used these facilities before and have never abused the privilege, and, furthermore, before we left, we scrubbed everything and left things in better shape than we found them."

The minister had the grace to apologize, and Eula went on her way. But it was most difficult to explain to these boys, who had known something was wrong all the time, the sort of religion that would not only tolerate but condone such actions.

"If a man love not his brother, whom he hath seen, how can he love God, whom he hath not seen?"

On a tour in California "The Cotton Blossoms" were invited to appear at a well-known service club's convention which was held on the West Coast. A program, composed of international music, was to be given to celebrate "Music Week." Just as Eula was preparing to herd her singers into the auditorium, a message was delivered to her from the chairman of the program committee which read, "Please remember to bring *your* flag when you appear on the stage."

"Your flag!" Eula was stunned. She did not know whether to laugh or weep. What, exactly, was their flag? What did the woman who knew exactly where they were from expect? The flag of Africa? She felt a wave of nausea go over her, then tried to get hold of herself, so that she would not tell the boys. But this was one time when "Papa" Jones's words came through in an extremely feeble whisper. She and the boys went on the stage and finished their singing, then she turned to the audience.

"I was told this afternoon," she began, her voice clear and sure as it carried out over the packed auditorium, "to be certain when we appeared this afternoon to bring our flag. I tried to figure out just what was meant by the request, and what, exactly, our flag was supposed to be. So far as I know the American Negro has only had one flag—a flag for which he has willingly fought and died. A flag that represents to him a democracy that he is willing to die for, in the hope that the Negro children in the future may achieve the freedom that that democracy has promised us. It is a flag we all serve, willingly, though none of us expect to attain that freedom that it symbolizes within our own lifetime. It is the only flag we have."

When Eula walked off the stage there was at first a stunned silence, and then a thunderous applause broke out that shook the building. Men and women crowded around her to offer their apologies.

Back at Piney Woods, Eula, as she knew she would, confessed to

"Papa" Jones, and then waited to see what punishment he meted out. He only shook his head sadly. "I don't know that I would have done it," he said, "but I don't find it in my heart to blame you."

Actually, in operating the way that he did, Jones's methods were simple but subtle. He aligned with men of good will and good faith, and caught the others "where their souls were short." There were many good men of every faith whose hearts were equally torn by a religion of the "mouth out" rather than of the spirit, in which so many so-called "men of God" stood still to insure their popularity rather than move forward with the world toward the tenets of Christianity.

Once when Jones was invited, with a quartette of his boys, to appear at a church supper in a southern town, the pastor told him that he wished to entertain the Piney Woods group at supper before the program. Not wanting to see the good man jeopardize his job, Jones suggested that he and his group would eat before they came.

"No," the minister insisted, "I won't have it that way and I think I can work it so everything will be all right."

With some doubts, Jones agreed, and he and his singers arrived at the church before supper. The minister met them in the back of the church, hustled them into a little room back of the pulpit, and said, "Wait right here until I motion to you to come in on the platform."

The minister took his place in the pulpit and launched the evening services with a forceful prayer on the true meaning of the brotherhood of man, the direct rules for Christian conduct as they appeared in the Bible. He concluded:

"And He said, 'Love thy brother as thyself,' regardless of race, creed, or color. . . .'" At that moment the pastor signaled with his hand, and Jones appeared at his side, followed by his singers. The pastor quickly ended his prayer, then said, "Now we will all go in to supper." He led the way to the room where supper was to be served, with Jones at his side. His white southern congregation sat down to eat with "colored" folks without a protest, for had it not been, after all, at the urging of the Master?

Through his constant contact with the public, in behalf of his school, Jones had found through the years an interesting balance between good and evil. For every discouraging incident, usually caused by ignorance or prejudice, there appeared, often as if miraculously, a corresponding gesture of generosity or humanity to lift the heart and give courage for the future.

Travel provided Jones with his bitterest experience in prejudices. After the big railroads took over many of the smaller ones, the discriminatory practices decreased, but not altogether. Although the ticket window became less of a bugaboo, something could always happen on the train itself. There was a time when on the dining car Jones had a newspaper before him when someone was seated across the table from him. When he finally put the paper down, a man, who already had his bacon and eggs, jumped angrily to his feet and stomped out. And there still continued that lack of a room, the last one just taken, in many of the hotels. But year by year the discriminations became less and less, and to Jones this was most encouraging.

However, one trip that he made just before World War II proved nearly fatal. Jones had been given a letter of introduction to a man in a little northern town, got off the train late in the afternoon, checked in at the only local hotel, went to see his man, got his donation, stopped for a bite to eat, and through a rising blizzard trudged back to the hotel, tired and worn out, thinking only of a hot bath and a good sleep. As he started for the stairs, there being no elevator in the hotel, the man at the desk called to him. Jones went to the desk.

"I'm sorry," the man said, "but we have no rooms."

"But I've already checked in," said Jones.

"I am the manager," the man said, "and my clerk made an error and assigned you a room without proper procedure."

"If you will look," Jones said, "you will find that I have already signed the register, that I was properly checked in, and that there was no error."

"What is your name?" asked the man.

"Laurence Clifton Jones."

The man looked at the old-time register for too long a time, shook his head, and said, "I'm sorry, your name is not here."

"May I look?" Jones asked politely, turning the book around and looking at the place where he knew he had signed. His name, written with a pencil, had been erased and there was another signature over it.

"I see what was done," he said quietly, "but I believe you will find my bag in that room."

"Your bag is right over there," the man said, "right where you left it."

Sure enough, the bag was by the door, and outside the driving sleet and snow had increased in intensity.

"I will take any sort of room," Jones said.

"We have no space, none at all."

"There are no other hotels in this town," Jones said, "and the last train has gone. What am I to do?"

"I'm sorry, but I can't help you."

In desperation Jones told him about his school, what he was doing, and did his best to stir up some interest. But neither in the man nor in other people who had gathered around was there the slightest bit of sympathy.

"Anyhow," said the manager, winking to someone back of Jones, "it is just as well that we do not have space here because if you are half so important as you say, my hotel wouldn't be good enough for you."

Jones picked up his bag, buttoned his coat tight around his throat, and went out into the storm. He was a block away before it occurred to him that he might have tried to contact the man he had talked to that afternoon. Too late now. He pushed on, looking for a drugstore, something open, that he could get into out of the bitter wind that drove its icy prongs right through the marrow of the bone. But nothing was open. His experience before had taught him that it would be no use to go to the railroad station in a town of this size as the waiting room was invariably locked up to keep bums from using it.

A colored man battling his way along a street through a stormy winter night is an ordinary sight, but any man battling his way along a storm-swept street to keep from freezing to death is a tragic symbol of man's inhumanity to man.

Occasionally the wind stopped blowing for a moment—a strange, menacing silence as if it was preparing for something worse—then came blasts of icy sleet that stung his face like sprinkled acid. As he slid and fought his way along, hardly knowing where he went or what lay ahead, Jones had an almost uncontrollable urge to let out a fierce cry—something stranger and louder than the sound of the blizzard—that might drive through to the heart of humanity and force its attention on what was happening. But that, he realized, might bring a policeman and cause his arrest. Rather than face that, he would freeze.

As he came out under an arc light, at the intersection of two of the main business streets, he saw a figure emerge from the darkness of the blizzard—a tall figure in a fur coat and cap which obliterated his face. As they passed he thought that he felt a keen flash of interest in the man's glance. A moment later he faintly heard a voice above the noise of the storm, and then he felt someone behind him seize his arm. He swung around to face the man he had just met.

"Yelled at you to wait," the man shouted, "but couldn't make you hear me in this devilish wind. Stranger here, I see?" His eyes, as they glowed on him through the storm, were, like his voice, comprehensive, authoritative, but kind and full of reassurance. "Where are you stopping?"

"I'm not stopping," Jones shouted hoarsely in reply. "I have to keep moving to keep from freezing."

"Come along with me. I can put you up."

He led the way to his place of business, a furniture store, which had an office and a sitting room in the back. The man turned on a light and then busied himself building a fire in a big base-burner, working deftly and with few words. When the fire burned to his satisfaction, he disappeared into a storeroom and came back loaded with blankets and pillows and soon had arranged, on a big davenport, as cozy and comfortable a resting place as could have been found in a good hotel.

"Coal bucket is here," he told Jones, "and you can keep your fire up. I'll be back in a few moments."

He hurried out, and when he returned he had a wicker basket covered up with a napkin. "Thought you might need this," he said. "I'll see you in the morning."

Jones lifted the napkin from the basket and found a warm plate dinner which the man had evidently brought from a restaurant. He set the food out on the desk, settled down to eat, looked around at his snug quarters, with its glowing fire, and warm bed waiting, and marveled along with the wise and witty Portia, "how far a single good deed shines in a naughty world."

Chapter 21

"Jus' Let 'Em Know They're Human"

During a tour in the fall of 1941 a group of "Cotton Blossoms" appeared in a church near the campus of Upper Iowa University at Fayette. In the audience that night was a small, energetic professor of English named Dr. Zilpha Chandler. Charmed by the simple beauty of the spirituals, Dr. Chandler was also fascinated by the practical approach to education that the singers described at Piney Woods. Some time later she received a letter from a Piney Woods student asking for help to pay her tuition. Dr. Chandler answered the letter, asking the writer to tell more about herself, her studies, and what she wanted to do in life. The girl—the youngest of Pa Collins's brood which had by now expanded to fourteen—answered promptly and to Dr. Chandler's satisfaction. The teacher sent the tuition in installments.

The following spring Jones asked Dr. Chandler to make the commencement address at Piney Woods. She had never been South or visited a Negro school, and the invitation gave her both a chance to see at firsthand what was actually done there and stirred in her a latent sense of adventure. Actually her acquaintance with colored people had been limited to a hunter who had come each year to rid the Iowa farm community, where she had lived as a child, of wolves, and as a result she had vaguely associated Negroes with hunting, fishing, and hound dogs.

As she cautiously descended the train steps that spring day at the little Braxton stop, a jovial colored man with a playfully aggrieved smile on his face, ambled up, saying, "You Dr. Chandler? I hope you realize you've spoiled my fishing trip!"

It was the husband of one of the school matrons—a man who liked to fish in his spare time when he wasn't recruited, as now, for a school errand.

171

He piled the teacher's bags in a pickup truck and headed up the gravel road through its avenue of tall pines toward the school. When they wound around the last curve and the circle of campus buildings burst into view, Dr. Chandler stared with delight as big, black, genial Miss Ella Gant, chief matron for the boys, nodded and sauntered past, with a couple of dogs trailing at her heels.

To the little teacher, fresh from the rarefied atmosphere of a northern university, this introduction had all the earmarks of an exciting adventure. After one brief trip back to Iowa to make arrangements about resigning her job, she returned, for mere living expenses, to head the English department at Piney Woods and participate in the "sanest education and truest sense of values I have ever encountered."

As local school facilities in the Piney Woods area had gradually expanded to include full eight-year grade schools and an occasional high school for colored children, Piney Woods had increasingly accented its high school work, and added a junior college department, so that it now included fourteen grades. Dr. Chandler's college teaching background proved an excellent addition to the expanding program and she soon took over as director of the academic department, as well as teaching the high school and junior college English courses.

To stimulate her students' interest in English, Dr. Chandler turned her energies to building up the school's library facilities. There was no library building at Piney Woods, and what books the school had were stored, uncatalogued, in one corner of a classroom. Taking her cue from an old Piney Woods custom, Dr. Chandler began appealing to her friends back North for funds to build a library. As an experiment, she sent out some letters written as a classroom assignment by students in her English classes. Their direct sincerity proved to have an emotional appeal which was a key to people's hearts. More and more of these student letters—mimeographed for wider circulation—went out, to both North and South. When $10,000 had come in, ground was broken, and by the time the modern, well-lighted building, with both reading and study facilities, shelves, and card catalogues, was completed, more than $100,000 had been spent. which had arrived in contributions ranging from one penny to $10,000. More than two thousand white Southerners had contributed to the Piney Woods Library, heartening proof that the South was now interested in more than "cooking and plowing" education for its colored children.

Next Dr. Chandler turned her attention to the completion of a new academic building to replace old Goodwill Hall which had long outgrown its usefulness. A large donation had been set aside by Dr. Jones for this project, but Dr. Chandler was anxious to speed up the construction. Once more she used the words straight from the hearts of her students to hasten this fund, and already one floor has been completed, in which classes are being held. When the building is finished, it will provide a combined auditorium and gymnasium as well as modern classrooms.

Of her busy life at Piney Woods this radiant little teacher says, "Everyone works harder here than anywhere else I've been. Why, I do as much in two days as I used to do in a week. It's a way of life instead of a job."

Second in command to Dr. Chandler in her academic department, and to Dr. Jones, as vice-president and registrar of the school, is former Cotton Blossoms singer, Professor Singleton Bender. After finishing high-school work at Piney Woods, Bender went on, through a scholarship obtained for him by Dr. Jones, to graduate from Iowa State College at Ames, and then back to serve Piney Woods. Inducted into the army in 1942, Bender was commissioned a lieutenant and saw three and a half years of front-line action on the beachheads of Italy. Returning to Piney Woods following the war, Bender taught through the winters and spent his summers at Southern Illinois University working, with the aid of the GI bill, on his master's degree in educational administration, which he completed in 1954. With his Mississippi farm background, his many years close to Piney Woods, his gentle manner, and thoughtful approach to his work, Professor Bender is an able assistant to "Papa" Jones, whose chapel talks and personal encouragement, he said, "taught me more than anything I ever learned in books."

Another interesting addition to the Piney Woods "family" is ex-Chrysler official John Haien, who came to the school when he retired from Chrysler in 1953, to take over the job of works manager. Long active in youth work, Haien, under the aegis of K. T. Keller, had served as director of special training at Chrysler, a program designed to conduct youth activities among the children of Chrysler employees. Drawn by the sane practicality of Piney Woods' handling of underprivileged children, Haien made frequent trips to the school, finally built a cottage on Piney Woods grounds for himself and his wife, and moved in "at a dollar a year," to supervise, with good Dutch thrift, the school's dairy, farm lands, and farm equipment.

Of gruff, efficient Haien, Night watchman Kelly gave the local verdict: "When he first come down here, I says to myself, here's another damnyankee come down to raise co'n and raise hell. But you know, he's proved out! He's a fine man." Of Piney Woods Haien himself says, "I never saw a place where a man could better invest his life."

The spirit of Piney Woods which catches—and holds—both staff and students was well evidenced by an event which took place in 1950.

Dr. Jones received a letter from an old friend whom he had not heard from in many years. It was from John Webster who had read of the success of Piney Woods, and thought it might be of interest if he would write up some of his early remembrances of the school's beginnings and send the manuscript to Laurence.

The letter was postmarked at a town in Arkansas, and when Jones roughly estimated the years, he realized that John Webster must be approaching eighty. Jones immediately wrote that he would like for him to do this, but more important that he would be by to see him, on his way to the West Coast, in a week or so. This he did, and then word came back to Piney Woods to prepare a cottage on the campus, usually occupied by teachers but now vacant, for occupancy. When Jones returned to Piney Woods he had with him not the usual "ragged child," but Mr. and Mrs. Webster. Jones had found the old man friendless, ill, and "hankering" for one more look at the country in which he had spent his happiest days.

Severely crippled by arthritis, Webster had been bedfast for twenty years. Jones saw to it that his bed was placed in the cottage so that he could look out at the activity on the campus which he had contributed so generously to make possible. Each day the "little 'Fesser" dropped by to visit and talk over old times with his friend,

and whenever interesting visitors came to the campus, he steered
them by Webster's cottage for a chat.

The last year of the old man's life was spent in the comfortable
and affectionate surroundings of Piney Woods. Shortly before he
died, John Webster confided to one of the teachers:

"I wish I had had a son like Laurence Jones."

There is no effort made in the over-all operation of Piney Woods
to form a big, smooth-running machine out of an institution which
is primarily a "home" and a "way of life."

Through the years Jones has taken on "anyone who wants to
help," and he has never been known to fire a single person. If a staff
member is causing friction in one spot, he shuttles the person into
a less demanding position. Coupled with his singular patience is a
congenital inability to hurt anyone's feelings. One old, irascible
fellow, who wears a beret, beard, and temperament, because he once
made a trip to Paris, has been building an amphitheater for the
school for years. He wants to do it, and it will be an addition to the
campus if ever finished, but that his temper keeps anyone from
working with him so that it can be finished does not seem to Jones
an adequate reason for taking the project away from him "just to get
it done."

All in all there are more than forty members on the Piney Woods
staff ranging from old-timers such as Georgia Myers, and Mrs. Strat-
ton—the daughter of a Tuskegee chaplain who listened to young
Laurence Jones's talks of school, in Hinds County back in 1909 and
who after being widowed "came home" to help her friend—to the
vigorous young staff members, such as Miss Buckhalter and Mr.
Bender, who but recently switched from Piney Woods student to
Piney Woods professor.

They all share a common capacity for a phenomenal amount of
work and a common devotion to their boss and his school. As
Georgia Myers winsomely remarked, "The only time I don't come
when he calls is when I'm taking a bath in the wintertime!"

"What fascinates me since I have been in college work," said
"Papa" Jones's protégé, Dr. Oatis, "is the way he can draw good
people to him and then *hold* them. He's got two people on his staff
right now that I'd give anything to get hold of. They would completely balance my own faculty at Alcorn College. But even if I were

disloyal enough to try to get them, I know ahead of time that they wouldn't come."

Still basing his program on the theory that "an idle brain is the devil's workshop," Jones sees to it that the entire campus moves with an atmosphere of discipline, orderliness, and promptness. The students rise at 5 A.M. and go to their classes and jobs by bells. They march in line to their meals, and, if late, they get nothing to eat. During World War II many of the Piney Woods boys, when they went into service, wrote back saying how much that sense of order, discipline, and promptness meant when they entered the army. With such basic training behind them, they were graded ahead of other entries, and were thus able to secure advanced ratings.

Both the spiritual guidance and the special "discipline" problems of the students are Dr. Jones's province. Chapel services are firmly non-denominational, with the prayers led variously by himself, a rabbi, a priest, local ministers, and a group of young ministerial students from Mississippi College at Clinton.

Though Piney Woods has consistently taken students "just short of the reform school," less than a dozen have been expelled in the forty-five years of its existence, and there has not been a single police record by a former student.

Asked how they can handle with such success so many "bottom-rail" problem children, wise, kindly Miss Ella Gant who has been matron and nurse of the boys' dormitory since 1926 said, "We jus' let 'em know they're human."

"You've just got to *believe* in them," adds "Papa" Jones. As he rides or walks around the campus he has an eye out constantly for any signs of disturbance or trouble.

One girl, according to her teachers, made no adjustment or progress whatsoever. Whatever she was told to do, whether at work or in class, was met with stony indifference. Jones sensed that hers was the old familiar problem of the child who has known nothing but cotton-patch poverty and who lacks confidence. One morning he called the girl to him, then headed toward the garage back of the Community House.

"What you going to do?" she asked fearfully.

"Teach you to drive," he told her.

Paying no attention to her gasp of startled dismay, he got into the car and beckoned for her to do likewise. They went to a place away from the campus, where none could watch, and with infinite patience he explained what she must do to learn to run an automobile. The next day and the next they went through the same procedure. Within a couple of weeks she became a self-assured driver. In no time she was doing his chauffeuring for him and, with a driver's license, was sent out the next season to take one troupe of "The Cotton Blossoms" on a northern tour.

But the chief gain was in what it did to the girl's personality. Flushed with her newly acquired ability after a full season of driving a house car all over a country that she had never seen, when she came back in the fall she was ready to tackle anything.

"Papa" Jones never, if he can help it, permits the persecution of different shades of color by other shades among Negroes. On one trip to Miami, Florida, after making an address, as he was hurrying to his car he caught sight of a ring of boys and girls shouting invectives and shaming someone within the circle in a corner of a schoolyard. He hurried over and found that the group of dark-brown children had a little girl, almost white, penned up in spite of her frantic efforts to get out.

"Got a white daddy! Got a white daddy!" chanted her tormentors. "Don't know your daddy's name! Don't know your daddy's name!"

Dr. Jones elbowed his way through the outer circle, the members of which fled, took the little girl in his arms, and comforted her until she stopped her hysterical crying.

"Would you like to come with me?" he asked.

Through tear-studded eyes the child studied him a moment, then suddenly clasped him around the knees with thin, possessive arms as she sobbed, "Yes, oh, yes!"

"Papa" Jones found out where she lived, secured permission from her mother to take her to the school, and when he returned to Piney Woods a few days later he had a new "child."

A year later her mother died and the little girl grew up at Piney Woods. After finishing school, she took a business course and came back as his secretary. Eventually she married a minister and took up the normal role of wife and mother.

It does not occur to the "little 'Fesser" that any child is hopeless. On one occasion he brought back to Piney Woods a boy whom a local school had expelled as a "hopeless incorrigible." Under Jones's eye he straightened out, finished college, and later became principal of a large Negro high school.

Another girl at Piney Woods caused the staff so much trouble that she was nicknamed "the pest." When the rest of them insisted that she must be expelled because of her influence on the other students, Jones replied, "We'll see."

"You don't know this one," warned one of the teachers. "You have never seen such a poison personality. She won't respond to anything and she can't do anything."

On his first interview it looked as though the staff was right. Jones talked to her in his most persuasive tones from Shakespeare to automobiles, and only received a dull glance of indifference. For the moment he gave up, telling her to come back in a week, but in the meantime he made a point of singling her out and letting her know that he had a personal interest in her. But she evidenced no reaction. She did, however, come to his office the following week at the time he had set. Again he tried to arouse some spark, but to no avail. Then, banking on his belief that she could not have missed the fact that he had a sincere interest in her, he said, "If I wanted you to stay here with us, and your father asked you to come home and plant cotton, which would you do?"

"I'd go home," the girl said, " 'cause de Bible says to honor your father an' mother."

"Now you know," Jones said later to his staff as he reviewed the scene, "there must be some good in a girl who makes a statement like that."

With this one spark of faith to go on Jones kept working with her—talking, coaxing, stimulating, challenging. And in the end he won out. Gradually the girl developed an aptitude for her studies, finished Piney Woods, secured her degree in a northern university, and is now working on her master's degree at another university.

Following an article on Jones which appeared in *Reader's Digest* (in 1945) and was translated and carried in its Latin-American editions, a Señor Morales of Mexico City contacted Dr. Jones with a request to send his daughter to Piney Woods to learn English and to be given a practical education. Morales, a well-to-do businessman, sent the girl along as soon as Jones agreed, and was so struck with the training and education that she got, that he subsequently sent a niece, nephew, and all of the children of his employees to the school. Since he paid full board and tuition for his daughter, niece, and nephew, this not only helped out the school financially, but proved to be a splendid lesson in international good will for all of the students.

The spirit of the Piney Woods students is a refreshing treat to the white teachers accustomed to the more apathetic attitude of students for whom school is a "chore" rather than an opportunity. Mr. William Hutcherson, who comes out from Jackson to direct the band twice a week for a salary that roughly covers the cost of his gasoline, described, with happy amazement, how Piney Woods students do so much "with so little." The musical instruments have all been donated, and the students play whatever is available.

Hutcherson's time does not permit him to give individual instruction. "But while I am gone between classes," he said, "the first chair instruments work with the new members, rehearsing them so that they usually manage to keep up by the time I come back. They all have musical ability, but the thing that impresses me the most is their cooperation."

Mrs. W. Q. Sharp, a Jackson landscape artist, who first came to Piney Woods as an Art League member to schedule an art exhibition, ended up teaching an art class once a week. "We have so little time and so little to work with," she said, "and my classes change every season, but it is worth it just to give the ones who are interested an exposure to art and art appreciation. They respond so wonderfully—and they all show an amazing sense of rhythm and color."

That the Piney Woods method of preparing students, by lessons in "Christianity, character, and service," as well as in books, works has been eloquently proved. A Piney Woods graduate was the first farmer in the entire United States to pay off his FSA loan, which he did in two years rather than in the allowable forty. A barefoot boy from the cotton rows, who was doomed to a life of little more than field drudgery, and who came to the school without a cent— or a suit of underwear—became a captain in the United States Army in Korea, and now holds that rank in the infantry of the Regular Army.

Dr. Jones likes to tell about his "Jack Family" as the reverse of the sociologist's "Juke Family." While on a trip in the northern part of Rankin County he met the Jack family. The father and mother were "old-time teachers" who had brains, ambition, and six children, but who were utterly destitute and completely unable to do anything about the education of their "hostages to fortune." Dr. Jones was so impressed by the character of the parents and the potential of the children that he moved the entire family into an old vacant house on the campus.

The four boys and two girls all finished at Piney Woods with all of them and their parents "working their passage." One by one, as they graduated, they went North, and when the youngest child finished and joined the others, they lived in a seven-room apartment in Chicago, supported by their joint work. One of them became a postal employee, another a chef on the New York Central Railroad, another finished his doctorate at the University of Chicago and became a teacher, two of them became businessmen, and one girl eventually came back to teach in Mississippi and for the last sixteen years has been supervisor of four Negro high schools and thirteen grade schools in Scott County, Mississippi.

"My Jacks," boasted Dr. Jones proudly, "were at the bottom and rose to the top, every one of them. All that they needed was a chance."

Gertrude Buckhalter, a slim young woman with a dark, sweet dignity, skimped along as a day student at Piney Woods, with two days a week at home to help her mother do the washing and ironing for a white family at fifty cents a week, eventually graduated, went on to get a B.S. degree, and is now a full-fledged science teacher in Piney Woods academic department.

The records up to and including 1953 show that Piney Woods has turned out more than five hundred high school and more than a thousand junior college graduates who have gone into careers as farmers, businessmen, druggists, teachers, ministers, social workers, musicians, and nurses. More than twenty of their graduates are professional singers.

This is only the primary benefit of the school. A much greater result will come from the descendants of this group who will, in turn, want to be more than poverty-stricken field workers. Already the old graduates are flocking back with their daughters and sons to put them into "Papa" Jones's family. Just how they feel about this one-time home of theirs is evidenced by a graduate, David Ross, who is chef on the Pittsburgh Steamship Line. In the off season he comes back to Piney Woods to direct the school kitchen and to instruct the students in the "special tricks" of his trade. He has further shown his faith in the school by enrolling his three sons.

A Birmingham, Alabama, newspaper, in a recent survey of agriculture in the South, reported that almost without exception, where the houses were painted, the stock improved, and the crops diversified, there lived a farmer who had attended Piney Woods School.

Over and over they tell about what the school meant to them.

"The thing I remember," said Robert E. Lee, now county agent in the Delta region, "is that Dr. Jones was always available when any of us had a problem, and that no student ever left Piney Woods for the lack of money."

A barefoot boy who couldn't read or write or figure when he came to Piney Woods at the age of fourteen and is now a vocational trade teacher with three children of his own, two of whom he has sent through college, smiled wryly. "My family don't believe me when I tell them how I walked five miles barefoot over icy ground to get the only schooling I had before I found Piney Woods," he said. "I don't count myself a great success now, but I know what a long way I have come since I first heard of Professor Jones."

While it is evidence like this of R. P. McGee's that points up the practical value of the help, it is the heartbreaking example of a little girl now in Piney Woods who reaped the troubles of a broken home and the cruelties of a sadistic stepmother that underscores it.

"I was mos' dead when Dr. Jones found me and brought me to Piney Woods." She looked up, her eyes round with solemn sincerity. "I owe him my life or as much as my life."

There are hundreds who do.

Chapter 22

"Go Tell It to the Mountains"

Dr. Jones likes to tell the story about the farmer who was gazing at a field which he had cleared and planted, and which was now showing its first green promise of a healthy crop, when a stranger, chancing by, stopped to look admiringly at the fine young wheat and remarked, "Just see what God has wrought!" To which the old farmer replied, with tart realism, "You should have seen it last year when the Lord had it all to Himself!"

Considering the forty-five years of its existence, the original need that led to the founding of Piney Woods has not basically changed. The 1954 per capita income of Mississippi was less than $900 per year, despite the fact that this included the rich delta planters, the business incomes from cities as prosperous as Jackson, Greenville, and Gulfport.

On opening day the students pour into Piney Woods, as they have always done, on muleback, in farm wagons, old pickup trucks, and afoot, frequently with their possessions tied in a bandana, or wearing all the clothes they own. They come from poverty-stricken homes, from homes broken by divorce and death, from grandparents too old to care for them, or from older brothers, sisters, aunts, and uncles. Few of them have any money. And practically none would have any other chance for an education. One girl this year described with touching simplicity how "Mama went to school when it rained"—her only opportunity being when it was too wet to get into the fields.

Of the present enrollment of five hundred students less than 10 per cent were able to pay any tuition at all. It is a rule of the school that every student must do some work, and the majority are full work students. Of those who enroll 75 per cent graduate with an accredited high-school or junior-college diploma.

Two thirds of the students and all of the faculty live on the campus, in dormitories and cottages, that are a part of the modern $750,000 school plant. It has its own second-class post office, operated by Postmistress Nellie Jones Bass, who has remained at the school most of her life with the exception of a business course in Iowa, and whose husband, a Piney Woods graduate, is a captain in the Regular Army, and whose daughter is now working on her doctorate at Columbia University, preparatory to returning to Piney Woods.

Clothes are cleaned in the campus cleaning plant (one of the trade courses offered for boys), washing, sewing and ironing are done in the girls' classes, maintenance on all buildings is done by student labor, and the school's 1,600 acres, with its modern dairy, orchards, truck and general farms, produce 60 per cent of all the food consumed. Forty gallons of milk in the morning and thirty at night are separated, the cream churned into butter with a yield of seventy-five to a hundred pounds a week. Pitchers of fresh buttermilk and sweet milk are on the students' tables each meal, and they are free to drink what they want. Chickens furnish a good supply of eggs and an occasional Sunday dinner. Meat comes from the butchering of pigs and cattle from the school droves and herds. Homemade syrup is made right on the campus from the school's own cane and a grist mill grinds its corn, as well as that of neighboring farmers, into meal.

Girls are taught pressure-cooker canning for both fruits and vegetables, and more than twenty thousand quarts of both fruit and vegetables are put up each year.

Practical secretarial work is learned in the school office, after typing and shorthand classes, by helping out the eight paid members of the office staff. The reception office, where school visitors are greeted, is in charge of Mr. C. E. Dishman, a cousin of Dr. Jones who, after considerable wheedling from the "little 'Fesser," left a good job in the North to come to Piney Woods in 1929, and stayed on as office manager and secretary to the board of trustees, and to marry a charming and energetic Mississippian, Fisk graduate Mrs. Bertha J. Dishman, who directs the choir, has charge of the Honor Society, supervises Lunky Day, and serves as corresponding secretary for the school.

Eula Kelly Moman, in addition to supervising Community House and serving as official hostess for the school, fills an office job as school treasurer, dean of women students, supervisor of girls' industries, and handles all correspondence between parents of students and the school.

Then there is Mrs. Hooker, who came to study art and stayed on as bookkeeper, and whose husband is in charge of the dairy. Miss Allie Nimock, crippled by the loss of a leg, remembers when Dr. Jones "picked her up" and brought her to Piney Woods and when she graduated, sent her on to Tuskegee and then to the University of Southern Illinois, from which she returned to Piney Woods to teach typing and shorthand.

In charge of the endless circularization of donors, the getting up and mailing of *The Pine Torch*, the bookings of Dr. Jones, the school singers and the band, as well as handling all Dr. Jones's personal correspondence, is "the Boss," Mrs. Carrie Crofton, Dr. Jones's petite and indefatigable secretary who came to Piney Woods as a child of twelve and never left. Another of Dr. Jones's corps of secretaries (who handle all the subscription work as well as his own mountainous correspondence), Miss Doris Grisham is in charge of mailing out the carefully audited receipts to all the donors, as well as the letters of thanks.

Within the past few years the outside world has begun to take note of the results of the Piney Woods experiment.

A Mississippi newspaper reported in 1951 that "the Piney Woods School in Rankin County has meant much to the colored race. When you think of crime and any grave conflict between the whites and colored, you won't find the names of people of that institution being connected with it."

A year later a southern newspaperman, after a national tour, reported that Jones was the most frequently asked about of any Mississippian.

In 1952, when an article on Jones by Beatrice Plumb in the *Christian Herald* caught the eye of an alert government official the Piney Woods story was picked up by the State Department to use in the overseas information service as an example of democracy in action.

Then in December 1954 Jones received national recognition on the secretly planned "This Is Your Life" program. Out in California on a lecture tour, Jones was a little surprised on that particular Wednesday night that his hosts should insist on hustling him to a "show" on the way to supper. Polite as usual, Jones allowed himself to be taken to the "play"—sighed resignedly as they walked in to a packed studio, then quietly figured his host must have "really greased that usher's palm" when he found they were led to seats in a front row despite the crowd. The first laugh of the evening came when Ralph Edwards "dropped" "This Is Your Life" book in Jones's lap, showed the dignified gray-haired scholar his last name in gold letters, to which Jones replied, "Must be some other Jones."

Eventually convinced that it was not, Dr. Jones found himself being led onstage, where, one by one, came voices out of the past and present. The second big laugh of the evening occurred when he looked up to find hard-working Dr. Chandler right there in a Hollywood studio and muttered, in amazement, "Who's doing your work at Piney Woods?"

The old circle was at work, only now it reached out, by the way of TV cameras, to the hearts of people the country over. The Jones saga had an impelling sincerity of truth. That normally glib, smooth-talking Ralph Edwards was himself "captured" by the story, came through in an unprecedented and unrehearsed "pitch" toward the raising of a permanent fund for the Piney Woods School when he asked listeners to send in a dollar or whatever they wished to help out.

Money flooded into the little Piney Woods post office from south, west, east, and north in sums from a dollar to a hundred. As Jones walked out of the studio that night of the performance mailboxes were already being stuffed with contributions. Also dollars were pressed into Jones's hand as well as a check for $25 from a TV writer who had worked on the show, with the remark, "Here's $25 I can't afford—that's what I get for *watching* the darn thing!"

By the end of the first week $150,000 had poured into Piney Woods; two weeks later it had passed the $600,000 mark—a sure sign that people the country over felt Piney Woods was "worth keeping alive."

Back in Jackson a special program was gotten up in honor of Dr. Jones. To the outsider, this meeting, with its many "tribute

speeches," its response by the honored guest, was little more than
any memorial tribute to a job well done. But for the citizens of
Mississippi it was a revolution of love. For a sight without precedent
in the annals of this southern state took place as the row of speakers
on the platform included both white and colored.*

To many an emotional liberal and eager Negro the patient inch-
by-inch process which Dr. Jones has pursued to achieve his present
position of respect and good will would not appear "worth the
whistle." But for Jones it was the only possible way. "No race," says
Jones, "has yet been able to master the superiority complex. Its fall
may not be by the sword, but by the more subtle method of human
hearts crying out to human hearts." The more subtle method has
always appeared to him as the way that would insure the most lasting
results.

As he has so often done during the long years of painful growth
of his school, Jones judges the position attained in comparison with
what *was* and is thus able to take heart and have hopes for better
things in the future.

"When I first came to Mississippi," he explains, "an educated
Negro had best keep to the back roads, or under cover, if he wanted
to stay in these parts. Nowadays the whites complain if we don't
want to be educated. Then, a Negro who painted his house or fixed
up his yard was called 'uppity'—the whites' scornful word for Negro
ambition. Now, our white neighbors desire that we appear as neat
and as prosperous as possible."

When white people first offered their services to teach at Piney
Woods "we considered it dangerous for our neighbors to learn that
they were to be here permanently." Now the community around
Piney Woods not only knows, but approves, of the mixed staff and
of the many white visitors and friends who come to the school.

---

* Participants in the Jackson Memorial program in honor of Dr. Jones
were: Governor Hugh White, Dr. H. M. Ivy (chairman board of trustees for
Institutions of Higher Learning), Dr. P. H. Easom (director Negro educa-
tion in Mississippi), Hon. Ben Cameron (federal judge, U. S. Court of
Appeals), Mrs. Katherine Bellaman, Mr. and Mrs. W. J. Hobby, Mr. and
Mrs. W. F. Mahaffey, Mr. Bryant Horner (representing mayor of Jackson),
Mr. H. A. Brandt, and presidents of Negro colleges: Dr. J. S. Reddix, Dr.
J. R. Oatis, J. H. White, and S. W. Miller.

To illustrate the change, on a personal level, Dr. Jones described how, in the old days, he gave up his firstclass seat the minute the train crossed the border of a southern state and he frequently had to stand up due to the crowded Jim Crow section when there were plenty of vacant seats in the white section. On a recent trip from New Orleans to Jackson he stood up most of the way, but it was because "white passengers all over the train recognized me and sent messages for me to come around to their seats or compartments to tell them about Piney Woods."

The same change is gradually working its way into politics. "In 1910," he said, "a white man who aligned himself with rights or justice for the Negro was a 'nigger lover'—which was considered a worse crime than 'killing a darky.' Any public stand in behalf of the Negro was political suicide. Now, our best politicians and white leaders openly champion the Negro cause with no harm shown in the ballot boxes."

This sort of progress may appear scandalously slow to the outsider, but to the Mississippi folk, with a 50-50 black-and-white population, their background of slavery and economic bondage, their ancestoral remembrance of Reconstruction, their fears and hates lashed into flame by unscrupulous demagogues, the "inch-by-inch" process of becoming acquainted with their neighbors on a level of individual faith and good will points the way definitely toward a hopeful future.

There is little danger any more that Jones or his school will be "tampered" with by white interference. As one old white man confided to him recently, "The po' white folks like you and the rich white folks like you, and down here when the po' whites and the rich whites both like you, why you can durn well do jes' what you please."

And Dr. Jones "pleases" to make the Piney Woods School a more potent part of American life. The road that he had traveled, from 1909 to that "mixed" platform in 1955, where colored and white joined to pay tribute to his life, is a longer step than most men are privileged to see within their own lifetime. It is as if the whole country had somehow, by osmosis, absorbed the "flavor" of his work.

And by April 1955, through one TV show, they had bet on him

to more than $625,000, which, added to a small endowment on hand, amounted to more than three quarters of a million dollars that went to establish, at the will of the board of trustees, the "Dr. Laurence C. Jones Foundation"* for the perpetuation of Piney Woods School.

A friend of his recently went into a Chicago bank to change a one-hundred-dollar bill into singles. "Why, don't you know," said the teller, "that all the gold has gone to Fort Knox and all the dollar bills have gone to Piney Woods?"

Although this fund may give the hard-working Dr. Jones a chance for a breather, it cannot be for long. It now takes $100,000 a year to run the school, and that old bugaboo of having to raise it each year still confronts him. What Jones does not want is for the friends of the school to think there is no more need for their donations. There is an even greater need.

Although Dr. Jones is past seventy, a recent medical checkup does not indicate there is any immediate chance of the school's being deprived of his unique services. "Just keep up the way you are," the doctor told him, "and you'll make one hundred and fifty!"

Jones still follows a hectic eight-to-eight schedule that would exhaust many a younger man. He is constantly on the move, his short, stocky figure (he has put on weight in the past few years), benign brown face, and silvery head a landmark on the campus of Piney Woods, where he can be seen at all hours hastening from building to building as he directs, manages, confers, and stops to chat with children, students, visitors, and his staff. Except for breakfast and dinner (he does not eat lunch) he can rarely be found sitting still—even in his office where he goes to check up on his multitudinous mail, make plans for future trips, lecture engagements, and other activities.

During the past few years Jones has set up, in so far as it is possible, through his board of trustees, arrangements so that Piney

---

* Those participating in the celebration of the Piney Woods Foundation were: Bishop Duncan Gray, Rabbi Perry Nussbaum, Right Rev. Monsignor Joseph Brunini, Governor Hugh White, Hon. J. G. Homes (Supreme Court of Mississippi), Dr. H. Ellis Finger, Dr. R. MacFerran Crowe, Mrs. Emma Rollins, Mr. A. Boyd Campbell (president of U. S. Chamber of Commerce), Dr. J. L. Reddix, Dr. J. R. Oatis, and Dr. J. H. White. Signing ceremony by Dr. Jones and W. M. Mounger of Jackson Bank & Trust Co.

Woods will continue. More and more he has tried to delegate his own work to staff members and imbue them all with the spirit in which the school was founded.

"We are all equipped to carry on the work of Piney Woods without him," explained Dr. Chandler. "What we will lack will be the inspiration."

But no doubt the spirit is there in every student-made brick and desk, in the tall pines themselves, in the old cedar tree, log cabin, and certainly it is expressed on the homemade plaques with their axioms nailed up where they are easily seen, to teach their daily lessons of life:

"The difference between stumbling blocks and steppingstones is the way you use them."

"Devote yourself to a worthy task; you can't fail to have a worthy life."

"Fame is vapor, popularity an accident; riches take wings—only one thing endures—that is character."

Of his own personal future Dr. Jones has no qualms. "I'll keep working as hard as I can as long as I can," he said.

To a man for whom God has been a hand-in-hand ally and prayer a daily habit, death holds no terrors. When the time comes, Jones can, with the triumphant joy of old Aunt Liza, "hise de window and let de dove come in" with few regrets for the earthly record he has made.

Index